W9-CSD-867

The Innovation Edge

Oliver Wight Publications, Inc.

EXECUTIVE BREAKTHROUGH SERIES

Breakthrough Partnering: Creating a
Collective Enterprise Advantage
by Patricia E. Moody

In the Age of the Real-Time Enterprise
by Tom Gunn (Available May 1994)

Infopartnering: The Ultimate Strategy for
Achieving Efficient Consumer Response
by Andre J. Martin (Available June 1994)

The Innovation Edge: Creating Strategic
Breakthroughs Using the Voice of the
Customer
by William Barnard and Thomas F. Wallace

**Planning & Control in the Age of Lean
Production**
by Darryl V. Landvater (Available April 1995)

Recreating the Workplace: The Pathway
to High Performance Work Systems
by Steven R. Rayner

Reengineering: Leveraging the Power of
Integrated Product Development
by V. Daniel Hunt

The Innovation Edge

**CREATING STRATEGIC
BREAKTHROUGHS USING THE
VOICE OF THE CUSTOMER**

*William Barnard
and Thomas F. Wallace*

omneo

An imprint of
Oliver Wight Publications, Inc.
85 Allen Martin Drive
Essex Junction, VT 05452

To Brenda and to Evelyn
For Their Support, Their Patience,
and Their Encouragement

Oliver Wight Publications books may be purchased for educational, business, or sales promotional use. For information, please call or write: Special Sales Department, Oliver Wight Publications, Inc., 85 Allen Martin Drive, Essex Junction, VT 05452. Telephone: (800) 343-0625 or (802) 878-8161; FAX: (802) 878-3384.

Library of Congress Catalog Card Number: 93-060670

ISBN: 0-939246-41-4

Text design by Joyce Weston

Printed on acid-free paper.

Manufactured in the United States of America.

10 9 8 7 6 5 4 3 2 1

Contents

List of Figures

Introduction

The Innovation Edge has been written for courageous executives who are not afraid to listen to the voice of the customer. It is not for the faint of heart. If you're comfortable with the status quo, you will almost certainly be uncomfortable with what's presented here.

Innovation is the opposite of the status quo. It means change, big changes, changes of the quantum leap variety. Innovation, properly executed, means success in the 1990s. So if you're not afraid of changing the way you and your peers do your jobs—if you're on the lookout for far better ways to do things—if you view the status quo as an enemy and new innovative approaches as your friend—read on. This book's for you.

The Innovation Edge presents a number of tools and techniques that can give you an enormous "leg up" on the competition. They will enable your company to do better—most often *far better*—in creating and keeping happy customers. Please note:

1. These tools are *new*, *leading edge*, and *breakthrough*. They are not old ideas repackaged and relabelled. The odds are quite high that your competitors are not using them and probably haven't even heard of them.
2. These tools are *easy to understand*. You don't have to be a rocket scientist or a brain surgeon to use them. The

underlying logic is simple and straightforward, and readily understandable by busy executives.

3. These tools are *proven.* They work in the executive suite. Top management teams in real-world organizations— large and small, public and private, service or products—are using these tools successfully. You will see how by reading the numerous examples cited.

A Disclaimer

In the pages that follow, you'll become acquainted with a company called "B&W Inc.," its CEO Charles Evans, and his executive staff. The B&W company in this book is fictitious; any resemblance to actual companies and/or their personnel is unintended and purely coincidental. On the other hand, this make-believe organization and its people are truly a composite of many of the companies and executive staffs we've worked with over the years. Good people in high pressure situations, doing their very best to make the right decisions, often without effective processes to help them.

Please Note: The term *Management Product* is a service mark of Barnard and Associates, Cincinnati, Ohio.

Acknowledgements

We owe special thanks to our superb team of reviewers, whose critiques and encouragement were invaluable. They are:

Bob Aron, Ph.D.,
Director, Product Engineering Training and Education, Motorola University.

John Baumann,
Chief Operating Officer,
Duro Manufacturing Company.

Doug Daetz,
Quality Management Methods,
Hewlett-Packard.

John Edholm,
VP Operations & Sales,
Pierce & Stevens.

Larry Gibson,
Affiliate,
Eric Marder & Associates.

Also, for lots of help along the way, we'd like to thank Charles Cormier of Boeing Canada, Mark Bailey and Jay Wolf from Hewlett-Packard, Sherry Bosserman and Jean Stoner of Motorola, Jim Childs and Darryl Landvater of Oliver Wight Publications, Chris Stiehl of Pacific Gas & Electric, Ron Pannesi from the University of North Carolina at Chapel Hill, and Hanan Polansky from the University of Rochester.

We've been privileged to work with a growing number of executives and managers in companies that have successfully implemented these processes, and we thank each and every one of them. We've observed how their use of these tools has resulted in a significant competitive advantage to their companies.

It's now our privilege to share the results of these experiences with you, the reader. We wrote *The Innovation Edge* specifically for the busy executive who's confronted with tight deadlines, too many things to do, too many things on his or her mind, and too little time.

We deliberately kept *The Innovation Edge* brief, and that wasn't easy; it could have been twice the size. One of our objectives was for this book to be easy to read, in one or two plane rides.

Another goal for this book: to influence you, the reader, to adopt these tools and use them in leading and managing your organization so that it becomes more highly focused on the customer, more innovative, and more successful.

Bill Barnard and Tom Wallace
Cincinnati, Ohio

The Innovation Edge

CHAPTER 1

Crisis in the Executive Suite

"The basic problem, gentlemen, is we're not going anywhere," said Frances Collier of B&W Inc. "I've been the VP of Finance here for the past seven years and all I've seen are no-growth numbers. Sales are up less than inflation, unit shipments are flat, profits are flat. Everything is flat except for market share and the stock price, both of which are down."

"Fran, you're right, but look at the bright side," replied Harold Simon, Vice President—Human Resources. "We've become more efficient internally thanks to things like Employee Involvement, Total Quality, and Just-in-Time. At least our efficiency gains are offsetting inflation. Otherwise profits would be heading downhill and we'd really be in deep yogurt. Don't you agree, Charlie?"

Charles Evans, the B&W chief executive officer, thought for a moment, then said: "I was thinking about the same thing this morning on the way in to work. But it seems to me there's good news and bad news. Over the last twenty years or so, all these great tools have been developed to help companies run better. And as you said, they've helped us a good bit; we're a lot more productive on the plant floor.

"But something's missing. The bad news is where are our new tools? Where are the better methods and processes for top management, to help us do a better job? You know what I think, Harry? I think most top management groups are still doing their jobs the way they did in 1960. We, and most executive groups, are trying to compete in the 1990s with outmoded processes. I think the Total Quality revolution has passed us by."

A fictional example—but Charlie's right, you know. There truly is a quality and productivity gap in the executive suite. This book has been written to help close that gap. In it, we'll identify and explain a number of leading-edge processes, available today, which have had a profound impact on how—and how well—senior management does its job.

This challenge is important, and it's urgent. New and better tools are needed, to help executives close this serious quality and productivity gap.

A disclaimer: we will not address topics such as developing the five-year plan, the preparation of the annual budget, how to conduct effective labor negotiations, or maintaining good relationships with the investment community. These activities, and others like them, are common knowledge. Rather, this book centers on *new* processes, which lead to success in the marketplace. Its focus is customer delight, which comes about through the development and delivery of innovative, breakthrough products and services.

For perspective, let's review some developments over the last quarter century. During this period, an enormous variety of superb tools has burst onto the industrial scene:

- Activity-Based Costing
- Automation

- Cellular manufacturing
- Customer partnering
- Design for Manufacturability
- High Performance Work Teams
- Just-in-Time
- Manufacturing Resource Planning
- People Empowerment
- Supplier Partnering
- Statistical Process Control

and many others.

Each one of these technologies, individually, can provide significant advantages to companies. Many of them, used in concert by a company, can yield enormous improvements in quality, productivity, and profitability. But they're not enough. By themselves, they won't enable a company to generate and sustain long-term increases in customer delight, market share, and profitability.

WHAT ABOUT TQM?

At this point, you may be wondering, "But what about TQM—Total Quality Management? Wasn't it supposed to be the ultimate answer?" Well, let's see.

Total Quality Management is not a specific technology or process. Rather it's an umbrella concept, based heavily on Total Quality *Control*, encompassing a number of tools, such as those cited above, which are typically seen as outside of the quality control/quality assurance field. As such, it's analogous to "world-class performance" or "excellence." Its results have been mixed.

A recent *New York Times* article was headlined: "TQM Yields Shoddy Results," and went on to say that the Total

Quality Management initiative had delivered far less than it promised. *The Wall Street Journal* stated in 1992 that TQM was not living up to its advance billing. *The International Quality Study* for 1992 reported that "a number of organizations are expending a tremendous amount of resources and energy on practices that have little or no impact for them."[1]

Conversely, TQM has done a great deal of good, giving impetus to a reengagement of senior management with operations. Twenty years ago, the prevailing mind-set was that the operational side of the business didn't merit much executive attention; it would "take care of itself." Now that's changed. Today, top management is giving more of its time, effort, and energy to the product, service, and operations aspects of the business. And that's good, but not good enough.

Top Management Has Been Neglected

The industrial renaissance of the late twentieth century— the "quality revolution"—has in a very real sense neglected the executive suite: the CEOs, presidents, general managers, and vice presidents. Initiatives wrapped around "excellence," or "TQM," or "world class" can help the organization as a whole, but although their benefits are certainly felt by senior management, most often these initiatives don't address the top management jobs. They don't contain breakthrough processes that directly help the executives do their jobs more productively and with higher quality.

Symptoms of a productivity and quality problem on Executive Row include a well-documented loss of entire industries to foreign competition, erosion of significant market share in others, a rush to send jobs offshore and only to bring them back later, a lack of focus on customers, and not managing proactively.

WHAT ABOUT REENGINEERING?

Recently we've seen a massive round of lay-offs, downsizing, and delayering. Some of this is necessary. What's unfortunate is the way in which it's so often done: after rather than before the fact; abruptly, not well planned and executed over time; crude cutting with a meat cleaver.

Frequently, an approach called "Business Process Reengineering" is used to facilitate the downsizing. The concept is solid; it says to eliminate unnecessary tasks, thereby streamlining the organization. As such, it's not a totally new idea—good systems and design work does this, and these have been around for years. Reengineering, however, adds an important element of focus and urgency to the process.

Our concern with reengineering is not with the process itself, but rather that it's being used all too often as a cover for taking a meat cleaver to the organization, eliminating many of the people, but not truly improving and streamlining the business processes that are in place.

Allowing organizations to become overstaffed and underutilized in the first place points to a deficiency in the decision-making process. Subsequent downsizing with a meat cleaver rather than a scalpel only compounds the problem. People with extensive knowledge of customers, products, and the industry are let go and are not replaced. Or they are replaced by lower-cost people without this important knowledge. This can seriously weaken the organization and sap its ability to provide superior customer service. It also causes great pain to the individuals affected.

Business process reengineering alone does not offer all the answers. Changing the culture is not enough. Becoming "world class" in the use of Total Quality processes is not enough. Something more is needed.

IMPORTANT TOOLS ARE MISSING

These problems we've identified are symptoms. The root cause lies in the inadequate decision-making processes used by most senior managers. These processes haven't changed much since the 1960s. Executives work on the business plan and the budget; they approve new products; they reorganize; they worry about customer complaints and in some cases become directly involved; they keep a close eye on the financial statements. Yes, they may have a computer terminal on their desks, and they may engage in some MBWA (Management By Walking Around). But the basics of the job aren't being done much differently from thirty (maybe even sixty) years ago.

Almost everything else in business has changed—enormously. Competitive pressures on quality, flexibility, customer delivery, product life cycle, cost and asset management are far higher today. Because the entire business cycle has accelerated, decisions must be made more rapidly—and with far greater validity. The "band width" for error in the top management decision-making process has become quite narrow. Decisions need to be made quickly, and they need to be made correctly—the first time.

But where are the tools to help the executive team do this? Where are the top management counterparts of Statistical Process Control and Concurrent Engineering, for example? There's no connection between the decision-making tools and processes used by most top management teams and the reality of the world around them.

The most urgent area in business today is to improve the quality and productivity of top management decision making. Only then will the superb technologies cited earlier—People Empowerment, Total Quality, automation, Supplier Partnering, High Performance Work Teams, Just-in-Time, and all the rest—be able to deliver real benefits. Only then will our industrial renaissance reach its full potential.

ELEMENTS OF INNOVATION

In addressing the quality and productivity gap in executive decision making, we'll emphasize four fundamental factors. We call these "elements of innovation," and they form the foundation for the processes presented.

Four Elements of Innovation

1. Customer Issues—Service, Delight, Meeting and Exceeding Their Expectations—need to be the prime mover of the business.
2. The Executive Team Produces Products.
3. Executive Productivity and the Quality of the Management Product Are Critical Competitive Variables.
4. The Executive Team Needs Superior Processes to Produce a Superior Product.

Let's discuss each of these essential elements.

Element #1. Customer Issues—Service, Delight, Meeting and Exceeding Their Expectations—Need to Be the Prime Mover of the Business. The importance of the customer must be a core belief. It must be accepted, internalized, and acted upon continuously in every department and at every level in the organization. The customer's overriding importance should drive all of the company's strategies, tactics, new product development activities, improvement initiatives, and day-to-day operations.

> **MYTH: In business, job 1 is the bottom line.**
>
> **FACT: If a company's main focus is on the bottom line, then the bottom line won't be as good as it could be—and should be.**

Myths are powerful and pervasive. Even if they are untrue, they can motivate beliefs and behavior, because they have the appearance of being factual. In a 1990 survey of American CEOs, 73 percent said that American business is committed to quality and 65 percent felt that American consumers didn't believe them. However, a follow-on survey of the consumers themselves found that 84 percent— *almost nine out of ten*—believe that management is more concerned with profits than with delivering quality products and services.[2]

Customer Delight. The customers have the ultimate vote—their dollars—and too often they vote for products made by foreign companies who set delighting the customer as job 1.

You may have noticed we're using the term "delight" rather than "satisfaction" when discussing what an organization must provide to its customers. The reason: customer satisfaction is an inadequate goal; it's an obsolete concept.

ANCIENT THINKING	Customer Tolerance: Customers are a necessary evil.

1980s THINKING	Customer Satisfaction: Do what is currently being done, but do it better so the customers are satisfied.
STATE-OF-THE-ART THINKING	Customer Delight: Do whatever it takes to delight the customers. Slay the sacred cows.

The fact is that customer delight is intimately linked with profitability: the greater the customer delight provided by a company, then the greater its profitability will be over the long run. There is solid data to back up this point, and it comes from the people at PIMS (Profit Impact of Market Strategy). They've been surveying business for over 20 years, and have developed a data base covering over 3,000 business units.

The PIMS numbers show that the top 20 percent of companies by creating customer delight ("perceived quality" is the term used by PIMS) are almost twice as profitable as the bottom 20 percent. Among the benefits accruing to companies that deliver superior customer satisfaction are:

- "stronger customer loyalty;
- more repeat purchases;
- less vulnerability to price wars;
- ability to command higher relative price without affecting share;
- lower marketing costs; and
- share improvements."[3]

Is it any wonder they're more profitable over the long run? With benefits like this, how could it be otherwise?

Corroboration for the PIMS findings comes from a U.K.-based research effort, which found that every 2 percent improvement in how customers rated a company's quality resulted in a 1 percent increase in return on investment.[4]

And what about the ultimate "external customer"—the stockholders, the owners of the business? How about their delight? Well, high profits should result in higher dividends and a higher share price—and of course they do. Peter Lynch, the most successful mutual fund manager of all time while at Fidelity Magellan, certainly qualifies as one of the best stock pickers in the world. He says: "Often there is no correlation between the success of a company's operations and the success of its stock over a few months or even a few years. *But in the long term, there is a 100% correlation between the success of a company and the success of its stock.*"[5] (Emphasis ours.)

We maintain that a high percentage—40 to 50%—of the executive group's time should be spent in understanding what the customers want, and how to fit the company's products and services to meet those wants. Virtually all other decisions should flow from that point. And this means, for many executives, that they'll need to become much more involved and engaged with customers and the company's product/service offerings.

Element #2: The Executive Team Produces Products. Just as operations people and others throughout the company produce physical product for the external customers, so the executive group produces intellectual product—primarily for its internal customers—known as the Management

Product. It consists of the strategies, plans, and decisions made by the top management team.

MYTH: Strategic planning is unique, unlike any other activity in business.

FACT: Strategy is the output of a process. It is subject to many of the same factors that apply to other production processes.

Top management produces a product, and therefore many of the issues—problems, opportunities, processes—that apply to the company's physical products can apply also to the management product.

Element #3: Executive Productivity and the Quality of the Management Product are Critical Competitive Variables. Competitive pressures allow little margin for error. Thus the top management team needs to be highly productive in its decision making, and the Management Product must be one of very high quality.

Let's take the case of two competing companies—Alpha Enterprises and Bravo Inc.—of about the same size, roughly equal in technological competence. They're about on a par in operational effectiveness, too, both having successfully implemented Total Quality, Just-in-Time, Concurrent Engineering, and People Empowerment.

However, Alpha's top managers are much more effective *in the quality and productivity of their decision making.* They consistently "bat for a higher average" than their counterparts in Bravo Inc.

Who will win the competitive race? Unless something changes, Alpha Enterprises will win, hands down. What happens to Bravo? They go out of business, or go through a painful "downsizing," or are acquired perhaps by a former competitor, or the top management team gets fired. Or all of the above.

Here are two real-world examples. Forty years ago, Boeing, Douglas, and Lockheed were approximately co-equal competitors in commercial airplanes. Today, Lockheed has exited the business; Douglas, after being acquired by McDonnell, is much smaller than Boeing and is not healthy; a new competitor, Airbus, has required massive government subsidies. Boeing is the preeminent player in this field. A fundamental reason for this is the quality and productivity of the decision making and leadership emanating from Boeing's executive group.

IBM, Digital Equipment, and Hewlett-Packard (HP) were neck and neck in the mid-range computer business during much of the 1980s. By 1993, HP enjoyed a clear lead over Digital. IBM's mid-range business (the AS400 computer), while strong, faced an uncertain future; it was increasingly threatened by the turmoil within IBM, caused in large measure by shortcomings in the quality and productivity of decision making at the highest levels within the company. In 1993, *Forbes* reported that Hewlett-Packard's market value (stock price times number of shares outstanding) "is now two-thirds that of IBM; in 1990 it was one-tenth IBM's."[6]

We could go on and on: Xerox vs. Kodak, Delta Airlines vs. Eastern, the Japanese auto and machine tool industries vs. the United States. We know these industries and these companies. We know the good ones, and the bad ones, and the ugly ones. We've known them as employees, as customers, as suppliers, and as stockholders. We know their people. Our conclusion: people's inherent capabilities and

drive to succeed differ little between the winning companies and the others. The fundamental difference lies in
the productivity of the executive group and the quality of
its Management Product.

*Element #4: The Executive Team Needs Superior Processes to
Produce a Superior Product.* On the plant floor, it's not
good enough just to "work harder." To outperform the
competition, it's necessary for production people and
others to "work smarter"—to use the best processes and
technologies they possibly can. High performance work
teams, Statistical Process Control, continuous improvement techniques, and the intelligent use of automation are
just a few examples of using leading-edge processes and
technologies to outperform the competition.

It's the same way in the executive suite. Effective tools,
techniques, and processes are necessary for the top management team. They're necessary for this team to produce
its Management Product more productively and with
higher quality than the competition.

> **MYTH: Decision making is a creative process, and you
> cannot systemize creativity.**
>
> **FACT: Better tools yield better outputs. They can fos-
> ter and nourish creativity.**

The better tools—the processes, the technologies—
exist. They are:

- *New, leading edge.* The chances are your competition
  isn't using these techniques. (If they are, and you're not,
  you're probably in trouble.) Most of these tools are less

than a dozen years old. They're being employed by companies that we believe qualify as leading edge: Hewlett-
Packard, Boeing, and Xerox are three we've already
mentioned. NCR,[7] Procter & Gamble, Cadillac, Pacific
Gas & Electric, and Black & Decker are also in this
category, among a growing number of others.

- *Practical and proven.* Despite their newness, they're not
theory. As we just pointed out, these processes have been
proven to work in the real world. (We'll provide examples
throughout the book.)

- *Easy to understand.* You don't need to be a rocket scientist to comprehend the underlying logic of these tools.
Although some are buttressed by substantial computer
number crunching, all are *inherently simple*—readily understood by busy executives who have better things to do
with their time than dig into lots of unnecessary complexity.

- *Often lead to breakthrough discoveries and decisions.* This
is the payoff, the "deliverable." The effective use of the
processes presented here has repeatedly yielded
quantum-leap results. They've helped decision makers
uncover fundamental issues—previously hidden—about
their customers, their strategies, their products, and their
projects. These tools have helped executive teams to
improve:
  - their productivity: more actionable decisions per unit
  of time and effort expended; and
  - the quality of their product: better decisions, ones that
  lead to customer delight, greater market share, and
  higher profitability.

- *Enhanced teamwork among the executive group.* The processes we'll describe will help to foster teamwork within
the ranks of top management. The executives really do

need to be a team, a high performance team capable of delivering an ultra-high-quality product. Most top management groups can use help in this area, and these tools can provide that help.

Now it's time to take a look at the processes that support the executive group in shaping its Management Product.

NEW PROCESSES FOR THE EXECUTIVE TEAM

These new processes enable the executive team to create the Management Product productively and with high quality. Despite their relative newness, they've been proven, time and time again, to yield superior, breakthrough results in at least three significant areas.

1. *Hearing and Understanding the Voice of the Customer.* The tools in this area are the essential bedrock, the foundation for all that follows. Given that customer delight is the prime mover of the business, it couldn't be any other way. Therefore, it's essential to capture the "voice of the customer" before strategies are formulated and deployed, before new products are launched, and before logistics plans are made. The voice of the customer refers to their wants and needs—both stated and unstated. It refers to how the product would make their hobbies, or their jobs, or their lives easier and more fulfilling.

But there's a problem here and it concerns shortcomings in traditional market research. The conventional wisdom says to ask the customers what they want, and they will tell you. Wrong. They can't tell you everything they want, and therein lies the need for new, breakthrough tools.

Customers can't tell you everything they want, for two reasons. First, they become so accustomed to certain things that they take them for granted; they no longer think about them. For example, in a market research focus group on automobiles, none of the participants would be likely to express a desire for doors, horns, and windshield wipers. These product attributes are *expected*; they're assumed to come with the product, automatically.

Second, customers can't express everything they want— because they don't know how to articulate it. The possibility of such an attribute hasn't yet entered their minds. Let's assume that the automotive focus group we mentioned occurred forty years ago. Probably no one would have mentioned cruise control as a desirable feature in a car. However, some of those same people, a few years later, may have bought cars very different from what they intended— simply because the car had cruise control. When they saw it, they said, "Aha! I simply have to have one of those." This is an example of an *exciting* product attribute—the providing of a want not articulated by the potential customers. When a product contains exciting features, it wins sales in the marketplace.

This same idea can apply to an entirely new product— the Chrysler minivans, the Mazda Miata—or to an entirely new category of product such as the Sony Walkman or the Hewlett-Packard Laser Jet printer.

The third kind of attribute is *expressed*. Customers will tell you about these: peppy, good handling, reliable, big trunk, etc. That's what you hear about in focus groups and in most of the other conventional market research techniques in use today. *And that's the fundamental problem with much of today's market research: it's biased toward the status quo.* It overfocuses on expressed wants, and misses many of the breakthrough discoveries.

Therefore, capturing the voice of the customer means

more than listening to what they're expressing. It means "getting inside their world," observing what attributes would be exciting to them—and thus leading them to a favorable purchase decision. In the next chapter, we'll be discussing in more detail some important new market research tools to do just that, including:

- *In-Context Customer Visits.* This approach focuses on how customers use the product, or competing products, in their own environment: on the job, at home, on the athletic field, and so forth. In-context visits are typically conducted by a company person together with the customer—observing, questioning, probing—to elicit the customer's likes and dislikes, problems, suggestions, and new ideas.

  Bill Brigden of NCR's highly successful automated teller machine business unit identifies in-context visits as one of the keys to their success: "The information we gathered via our in-context market research gave us insights which we could have gotten no other way. We developed a superior understanding of what our customers wanted and what their priorities are."

- *Choice Modeling.* Much of conventional market research measures customers' satisfaction against a theoretically perfect product or service (which of course doesn't exist). Choice Modeling,[8] however, identifies customers' relative satisfaction between real alternatives, ones that do exist. This is what determines choice, i.e., which combinations of benefits and features they will buy.

  Bill BonDurant from Hewlett-Packard, one of the world's leading market research professionals, cites HP's experience in bringing out a new generation of calculator.

Based on the initial design, a choice model simulation predicted a market share of less than 1 percent. This encouraged the development team to revise the product specifications, aligning them with customer purchase patterns per the choice model. The result: "After one year its sales were 250% of quota. Dealers cannot keep the product in stock. They sell it out as quickly as they receive it. The product carries along a significant amount of add-on sales for HP peripherals, making it one of the division's most successful new product launches." The product gained a near *20 percent market share*, in sharp contrast to the predicted share of less than 1 percent prior to the redesign triggered by the market research effort.

Obviously, it's not enough, to do a great job of capturing the voice of the customer. Once we hear what they're saying, we need to do something with that intelligence, and that brings us to the second of our new processes.

2. *Customer/Strategy Linking.* This imbeds the voice of the customer into the company's strategies. Given that customer delight is job 1, it's essential to have the company's plans and decision-making processes tightly linked to—and driven by—customer issues.

The Customer/Strategy Linking processes we'll describe in Chapters 3 and 4 are based on a methodology that originated in Japan called Quality Function Deployment (QFD). This approach, built around a powerful form of matrix analysis, enhances people's ability to imbed the voice of the customer into the design of products.

Companies such as Hewlett-Packard, Motorola, NCR, Pierce & Stevens, Procter & Gamble, and others have extended the use of the basic QFD tools (originally developed for product design purposes) into the executive suite, helping senior managers use this rigorous process to link the voice of the customer tightly into the development of the company's strategies, plans, and top-level decisions— the Management Product.

This is a radical departure from current practice. In most companies' strategic plans, customer satisfaction issues are conspicuous by their absence. In this situation, what are the chances that the company's people, no matter how well intentioned, will be able consistently to provide superior customer satisfaction? Perhaps slim or none. And the reason, of course, is that if the total organization isn't focused on customer delight, the odds are overwhelming that it won't happen.

But it's not enough just to produce a product, whether it be the physical product (or service) or the Management Product. The product has to be *delivered*, and that's the role of the third of our new processes.

3. *Strategy Deployment.* This process serves the important role of transmitting the strategies and their action plans throughout the organization, obtaining buy-in, and tracking progress toward their achievement. Strategy Deployment forms a major part of the "distribution system" for the Management Product. Customer/Strategy Linking helps executives to develop their product; Strategy Deployment helps to deliver it.

Strategy Deployment techniques are based on another Japanese development, this one called *Hoshin Kanri*.[9] In the English language, none of our terms adequately captures the essence of this structured process, which is to deploy strategies and their action plans with a high degree of buy-in from the people throughout the organization.

In many companies, this linkage is not tight; it's either loose or nonexistent. Thus the strategic plans are not effectively transformed into action. They either don't impact the real world at all, or do so only partially and ineffectively. The result is that the strategic planning exercise is just that, an exercise, rather than an important competitive weapon in the company's arsenal.

Effective tools to deploy strategies can make a huge difference. Charles Cormier, Director of Operations Support for Boeing Canada in Ontario, says: "It was tough at the beginning, involving dozens and dozens of people in strategic planning and decision making. But now we've grown into it, and we're getting better all the time. I simply can't see doing it any other way. We now have the assurance, with very high probability, that we'll accomplish our strategic goals."

This new process of developing and delivering the Management Product is shown graphically in Figure 1-1.

In many industries, product technology is an important competitive variable—but it is not a fundamental factor. This is often also true for process technology and automation. They are important but not fundamental.

In every industry, people-based technologies are critically important. However, as we saw with our fictional example of B&W Inc. at the start of this chapter, it's not enough to improve processes via Total Quality and Just-in-Time; it's not enough to change the culture via People Empowerment and teaming; it's not enough dramatically to reduce time to market via Concurrent Engineering and Design for Manufacturability. Yes, these are essential. But also required are breakthrough customer-driven decisions from top management, resulting in clear strategic directions communicated widely throughout the organization.

FIGURE 1-1: Developing and Delivering the Management Product

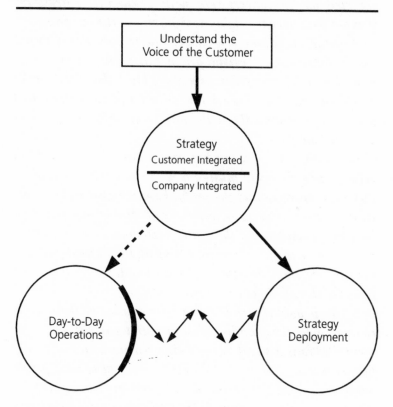

We believe that these three processes—Hearing and Understanding the Voice of the Customer, Customer/ Strategy Linking, and Strategy Deployment—are essential for breakthrough decision making and leadership. As such, they're essential for survival and success, because the quality and productivity of top management's decisions comprise the *fundamental competitive variable*.

Let's return to B&W Inc. and learn a bit more about their situation.

Later on that January day, the B&W CEO Charles Evans reflected on his conversation with Fran and Harry. He thought back over the eighty-year history of the company.

Founded in the southern United States as the B&W Pencil Works, the company's initial product line reflected the abundant sources of timber in its region. Over the years, B&W prospered and the product line broadened to include ball point pens, mechanical pencils and a broad offering of felt-tip pens and markers.

In recent years, growth has been hard to come by. Sales volume is in the $500 million a year range; unit volume is flat; gross margins and net profits have not grown. The company's conservative fiscal policies and strong balance sheet have kept it viable, but these same factors make it an attractive takeover target. Dividends have also remained flat over the past few years, and the stock price has declined 15 percent from its all-time high of the late 1980s.

B&W is publicly traded, but over a third of the stock is controlled by the founding families and current management. There is a small but growing sentiment among some family members to sell B&W. However, most of these people want the company to remain independent, fearing that a merger could result in significant job losses in the southern city where B&W is based.

The company is regarded by its employees and the community as a fine place to work and a good corporate citizen. The investment community feels it has value only as a takeover target. Its customers see it as a solid supplier of high-quality but not very exciting products. Most of its recent efforts in introducing new products have been viewed by the marketplace as "me-too," and they have not been successful.

The B&W executive group consists of:

Charles Evans	*CEO and President*
Frances Collier	*VP—Finance*
Harold Simon	*VP—Human Resources*
Michael Perez	*VP—Marketing & Sales*
Owen Barnes	*VP—Operations*
Paul Lewis	*VP—Product Development*

This group has been together for almost ten years, most of which have been reasonably harmonious. However, some of the executives sense that the stresses caused by recent lack of growth are taking their toll: they feel that finger pointing has increased, teamwork is not as visible, and meetings have become more contentious. To a person, though, they are loyal to the company and dedicated to its continued success. Keeping the company independent is a high priority for each of them.

"Doggone it!" thought Charlie. "We've got good people in our top management group, we're working really hard, and we all sure want this company to succeed. But it's not happening. We're letting the rest of the folks down—the managers and supervisors and the production associates and the people in the office. Unhappy customers and unhappy stockholders make for unhappy executives."

At this point he was interrupted by a visit from Michael Perez. "Charlie, I just got back from a seminar on new approaches to market research and strategy development," Mike said eagerly. "And I think maybe this might be a big piece of the puzzle as to why we're having trouble."

"How so?"

"Well," Mike went on, "I've got a feeling that we really don't know what our customers want. In fact, I'm not even sure we've got a good handle on who all of our customers are.

And I'm convinced that we don't know how and why they make the purchase decision.

"For years, Charlie, we've taken all this for granted. We were convinced we had all the answers here. But, if so, why have our new products bombed in the marketplace? That's the bad news. The good news is that I think there are tools out there that can fix our problem."

CHAPTER 2

Understanding the Voice of the Customer

"*Time out, Mike,*" *countered Charles Evans, CEO at B&W Pencil Works,* "*Are you telling me that all the money—the megabucks—we've been spending on market research has been wasted? That we don't know what our customers want and don't even know who they are? We've done surveys and focus groups till we're blue in the face. Michael, what did they feed you at that seminar?*"

"*Not all the money's been wasted, Charlie,*" *replied Mike.* "*We've got some good results from our market research over the years. It's helped us make some sensible decisions on which market segments we should be in and which we should stay out of. Remember when we were thinking about buying that paper company? I'm glad we had the sense to dodge that bullet.*

"*But I can see now that a lot of our market research hasn't done much except reinforce our own views of the customers. The problem is that what we believe about our customers hasn't changed for a long time; we still see them the same way. Am I right, Charlie?*"

"*I can't deny that, much as I might like to.*"

"Okay. Maybe—just maybe—our customers have changed. Hell, everything else in this crazy world is changing. Isn't it likely that our customer base has changed too: its composition, its needs, the way it uses our products?"

Just then the two men were joined by Owen Barnes, Vice President of Operations and a grandson of one of B&W's founders. He said, "One of the things they taught me at West Point is in battle to hold the high ground. So if you guys are having an argument, can I bet on Charlie to win?"

Charlie smiled. "Don't be so sure, Owen. Mike might be onto something here. He's got me wondering if we really do understand our customers."

"Well, I'll tell you guys, we could sure use some new business. Thanks to Just-in-Time and Total Quality and all the other good things, we're making the same volume with fewer people in less space. We've been reducing the workforce by attrition—haven't hired any new production people in ages," said Owen. "If the trend continues, we can start thinking about closing Plant 2. "We've got a world-class workforce and world-class facilities that are underutilized. It's like using the SST to shuttle between New York and Boston. We need some volume out there and we need some challenges."

Charlie thought a bit, then said: "Mike, how about if you take some time at the next staff meeting? Tell us what you think we should do about this issue of not knowing enough about our customers."

B&W may be starting to get on the right track. Consider the following:

MYTH: Companies know what their customers want.

FACT: "What people in any business think they know about customers and markets is more likely to be wrong than right."[1]

FACT: "The customers rarely buy what the business thinks it sells them."[2]

FACT: "Features regarded as most important by the producers may be relatively unimportant to the customer."[3]

FACT: "It is the customer who determines what a business is. What the customer thinks he is buying, what he considers 'value,' is decisive—it determines what a business is, what it produces and whether it will prosper."[4]

All of these quotes are by Peter Drucker, taken from the 1950s and 1960s. Just as with Deming's warnings about quality, Drucker's words about the central role of customers went largely unheeded by American industry. The good news is that now things are beginning to change.

The 1990s will go down in business history as the decade of the customer. Understanding customers—who they are and what delights them—is a primary survival issue for the 1990s and beyond. There's a real trap here, because most companies are *convinced* they know these things *cold*. It's ludicrous to suggest otherwise, they say, because "after all we've been selling to them for years." And for the same reason, they claim, "we know what they want." (Another key survival issue—in addition to knowing what the customers want—is *delivering* it. That topic will also be addressed throughout this book.)

Mike Perez from B&W hit the nail on the head: It's likely that the customers are changing, or perhaps the competition is changing for the better, or both. This issue comes down to two fundamental questions:

1. *Who are our customers?* Who really makes the purchase decision? Is there more than one person involved? Are there new people in the decision-making loop—or perhaps people in the loop have been there all along but have never been identified?
2. *Why do our customers buy?* On what basis do they make the purchase decision? What motivates them? What combination of product and service attributes makes them say yes—or no?

Being close to customers—understanding who they are, why they buy, and what the competition is doing to satisfy them—will increasingly be a survival issue, a matter of life or death for many companies. And the sad truth is that today most companies—those that do market research as well as those that don't—simply don't have a good enough handle on who their customers are and why they buy.

Experts' estimates of new product failure rates range from 80 to 95 percent. In other words, only about one new product in ten succeeds in the marketplace. The American Marketing Association estimated that only 5.7 percent of the 15,000 consumer package goods products introduced in 1992 were innovative[5]—and of course not all of that 5.7 percent were successful.

On the other hand Hewlett-Packard, a company that's superb at knowing its customers' wants and that uses virtually all the tools described in this book, has extremely high success rates with its new personal computer products.

MYTH: Traditional market research does an excellent job telling companies what they need to know about their customers.

FACT: Traditional market research techniques tend to reinforce the status quo. They rarely lead to innovative discoveries about what customers really want. As such, they are no more adequate for the 1990s than traditional approaches to production, quality, employee relations, supplier relations, and product costing.

Over the last twenty years, the industrial world has experienced a revolution in how companies operate. As we saw in the first chapter, a wide array of new tools, technologies, and processes has burst onto the scene. A company trying to compete without these superior tools is in the same position as a golfer on a pro tour today with a 1930s set of clubs in his bag. The golfer won't win any tournaments; he'll never even make the cut. This company won't win many orders; in time it won't make the "survival cut."

In the business world of the 1990s, the same old way won't work. *Market research is no exception.* The standard, traditional kinds of market research which have been practiced over the years frequently *average the responses received from customers.* The resulting "average customer" may in fact be unlike any of the customers in the real world. In much the same way that it's possible to drown in a river that has an average depth of one foot, companies will not succeed in the marketplace because of inaccurate assessments of their customers.

For example, if a beverage company's market research shows that half of those surveyed want a sweet drink and the other half prefer tangy, the worst approach would be to produce a product halfway in between.

Traditional market research tends to concentrate on *individual product attributes*, one at a time, rather than probing for which *combination of attributes* will lead the customer to buy—or not to buy. For example, one of the authors recently purchased a notebook computer. In response to a conventional market research questionnaire, he would have answered these kinds of questions:

Do you want high speed?	YES
Do you want a large disk?	YES
Do you want an easy-to-read screen?	YES
Do you want color?	YES
Do you want long battery life?	YES
Do you want light weight?	YES
Do you want a full-function keyboard?	YES
Do you want a built-in modem?	YES
Do you want a mouse or trackball?	YES

Unfortunately, the information listed here is inadequate to determine *how* he made his decision. If asked, he could have ranked the answers in order of preference. But that still wouldn't have gotten the job done.

He bought a machine with an average battery life, that wasn't the fastest, didn't have a particularly large disk, without a color screen, modem, and or a mouse. It wasn't any single attribute that determined his decision. Rather, he made his choice on the *interplay* of a variety of the features cited. It was a heavy compromise, certainly, and that fact alone may say something about the ability of notebook computer manufacturers to understand at least one segment of their customer base.

So the important question is not how well does the

"average customer" like this feature or that one. The real issue is which *combination of features* will match individual customers' choice patterns, and motivate them to buy. Frequently, traditional market research comes up short on this critically important question.

That's a problem, a big one. Very shortly we'll identify some solutions. But first we need to touch one other important base on this issue of customer decision making.

THE VALUE PROPOSITION

The value proposition recognizes the fact that, although price is important, few buying decisions are based on price alone. It further states that although the product's benefits are very important, they are seldom the sole determinant in the purchase decision. Rather, the decision to buy or not to buy is almost always based on an assessment—conscious or subconscious—of perceived benefits compared to price. The difference between perceived benefits and price is called "value." In equation form:

$$\text{VALUE} = \text{BENEFITS} - \text{PRICE}$$

If the difference between benefits and price is perceived to be high, the product or service has high value. Obviously people will be far more likely to buy a high-value product than one perceived to be of lower value.

But it's not *quite* that simple. This is where competitors rear their ugly heads, to offer the potential customer a range of choices, which can include different benefits or lower price. Thus the purchase decision is most often dependent upon product A's perceived value relative to those of product B, product C, and so on. This is how private-label consumer package goods have eroded the market share of major marketers such as Procter & Gamble and others. Unlike years ago, many private-label products today offer much the same set of benefits as the established brands, but their lower prices alter the relative value dramatically, and the customers have moved to them by the millions.

Thus the decision to buy or not to buy a given product is usually the result of a variety of product features and price points spanning a number of competing products. And all of these are colored by the buyer's *perception* of these attributes, which may or may not match closely with reality. A complex process indeed, but one that winning companies excel at understanding.

The Kano Model

To help with that understanding a Japanese academic, Noriaki Kano, developed what's called the Kano Model, a way of looking at product and service features and their impact on customer delight:

Basic Features: These are attributes of the product or service that do not generate positive satisfaction when provided, but do cause negative reactions when not provided. As we saw in the first chapter, this is sometimes called *expected* quality.

Competitive Features: These are attributes that cause increasing satisfaction the more they are provided, and cause increasing dissatisfaction the less they are provided. Referred to as *expressed* quality.

Excitement Features: These are attributes that create delight when provided, but cause no dissatisfaction when not provided. Often the customers aren't aware of the possibility of such a feature, and hence are delighted when it's provided. *Exciting* quality.

The challenge, of course, is in the third group: how to build exciting features into one's products and services. It's so difficult, because the customers can't tell you that they want it. They're not aware they want it until they see it.

Who Are Our Customers?

For many years, Bill Barnard has made an interesting offer to companies as he began to work with them on strategy and product QFD: he bet $100 that they didn't know who their customers are; more specifically, who all of their customers are for a specific product line. In over ninety QFD projects, he's never lost his bet.

How can this be? Surely companies can identify their customers. After all, they're all in the master file in the computer; just look them up.

Well, yes and no. Most companies do know who their "customers" are, current and potential. But within a given area, many companies simply haven't identified all of the people in the decision-making loop so far as buying the product is concerned. These decision makers must be sold, in one way or another, on the product's value.

Let's take the case of the Xerox machine in the Accounts Payable Department. The current one is starting to wear out, and it might be time to purchase a new unit. The customers for this potential purchase include people ranging from the end user to the installer, planner, and so-called intermediate users, as the following table shows:[6]

VIEWPOINT	DEFINITION	EXAMPLE
End user	Directly benefits from using the product	People who work in Accounts Payable, plus Payroll and Accounts Receivable with whom they share the machine
Operator	Provides resources and supplies to the product	The person in Accounts Payable who's responsible for keeping the copier supplied with paper, toner, etc.
Maintainer	Repairs the product	The maintenance person from the Office Services Department (or the office equipment dealer)
Installer	Integrates the product into its environment	The installation person from the office equipment dealer (or from the Office Services Department)
Auditor	Prevents misuse of the product	The manager of the Office Services Department, who is charged with ensuring that copy machines are used for business purposes
Funder	Pays for the product, its installation, operation, and maintenance	The General Accounting Manager

VIEWPOINT	DEFINITION	EXAMPLE
Planner	Determines consistency of the product with organizational policy	The Vice President of Administration, who is charged with having the proper number of copy machines in the right locations
Intermediate user #1 (e.g., retailer)	Directly benefits from the product but is not the end user	The owner or manager of the office equipment dealership
Intermediate user #2 (e.g., wholesaler)	Directly benefits from the product, but is not the end user nor next to the end user	The owner or manager of the office equipment distributorship

That's ten different categories of customers whose wants and desires need to be taken into account if the "voice of the customer" is to be captured completely. (Not all of these "customers" require direct selling efforts; in many cases, the important issue is to understand their needs and develop the product/service accordingly.) Most companies have a good handle on the needs and wants of several of their customer categories; very few really know what motivates all of their customers.

Why Do Customers Buy?

Here's Peter Drucker again: "Indeed, *what the customer considers value is so complicated that it can only be answered by the customer himself. Management should not even try to guess at it*—it should always go to the customer in a systematic quest for the answer.[7] (Emphasis ours)

Both authors have experience in kayaking, and one of the phenomena we've observed is the wide gap between paralysis-by-analysis and ready-fire-aim. For example, before running a difficult rapid, the kayaker has a choice: to scout or not to scout. In other words, study the rapid ahead of time and lay out the desired route; or, don't bother with scouting—just go ahead and run it. The latter approach, which might be called ready-fire-aim, is not recommended.

The proper way is to scout the run ahead of time, but not to excess. Overstudying, overanalyzing, overthinking could lead a kayaker into information overload. This could result in a decision to portage around (which may or may not be a good idea), or a confused, poorly planned run with unfortunate consequences. What's needed here is a *balanced* approach.

It's the same story in the business world. Ready-fire-aim is not, *repeat not*, the way to develop strategies or to launch new products; there's simply too much at stake. Paralysis-by-analysis doesn't work either; opportunities are missed and competitive advantage often goes to those who are quicker off the mark. The processes we'll discuss here represent a proper balance, one that might be called "ready-aim-fire."

These tools help to answer the very difficult but crucial question raised by Peter Drucker: What do the customers consider value; what leads them to buy? They are proven techniques that companies are using to make enormous impacts in the marketplace and on the bottom line.

Out of the wide array of existing market research techniques, we'll discuss three: focus groups; in-context customer visits; and Choice Modeling. The second two are relatively recent techniques, so we'll spend more time on them.

FOCUS GROUPS

This is a form of market research that's based on facilitated group discussions. A "focus group" is a panel of actual or potential customers, led by a moderator who elicits comments from the panel members. The results are normally qualitative, not quantitative.

Focus groups work well when used for the right objective: generating new ideas. As such, it's a blue-sky kind of process that occurs at the start of the attempt to understand the customer. "What's your routine when you get up in the morning?", "What could your personal computer do to make your life easier?", "Why do you hate your bank?" are the kinds of questions that should be asked in focus groups.

Focus groups don't work well when they're used for the wrong purpose: idea testing. The kind of question best *not* asked in a focus group is: "Here's our idea for a new product; how do you like it?" The resulting answers will tend to lack objectivity and thus can be very misleading.

One reason: most people try to be positive. They will tend to answer questions in a way that is friendly and supportive. In a focus group, the subjects know that they've been invited to discuss a topic that's important to the host organization. They've been given refreshments, and perhaps they'll be paid for their time. In this environment, the subjects' true feelings can be masked by the desire to be supportive and helpful, to reciprocate. This makes for a pleasant session, but not necessarily for good market research.

IN-CONTEXT CUSTOMER VISITS

In-context visits are quite different from other kinds of market research, in that they focus on customers in their own environment. This creates a significant advantage. In-context visits place the company person together with the customer in the setting where the product or service is used—the customer's "native habitat," so to speak. It's in this forum that both parties, working together, can identify current and future customer wants.

Some companies mistakenly believe that they already do in-context market research. "Sure we do," they'll say, "we visit our customers all the time. We make sales calls and if there's ever a major problem, we'll send in a few execs to make things right." This doesn't qualify as market research.

In-context visits are not sales calls, nor are they "firefighting" events. In fact, one of the more difficult aspects of the in-context process is to convince the customers that you're not trying to sell them anything (or to make alibis as to why the last three shipments were messed up). The dynamics of the in-context visit is one of observing, learning, dialoguing.

Some people would counter by saying that these activities—observing, learning, dialoguing—are the essence of a good sales call. And they would be right, but there are important differences, one being the *objective* of the visit. In a sales call, one objective is to convince the customer that the product is okay and that they should buy it. In-context visits focus instead on how we could make the customer's job—or life—easier, more productive, of higher quality, and so on.

An equally important difference is *structure*. In-context

visits are structured events, which means that customers' responses can be probed to obtain more specific, in-depth information—usually of a qualitative, not quantitative, nature.

A third difference can often be *location*. It's important to conduct the in-context visit on the customer's home turf. In our example of the copy machine in Accounts Payable, end users would be observed and interviewed at the actual point of use: the machine itself. The operator and the maintainer might be observed there, but also in ordering and receiving supplies. Auditors, funders, and planners would most likely be interviewed in their offices, while visits with the installer and intermediate users would occur at their companies.

A fourth difference is *data collection*. Successful users of in-context market research most often employ audio taping, and sometimes video taping. The tapes are transcribed, and the results of this are analyzed and evaluated. (There's good news here. Computerized tools can make this data reduction and analysis much less time-consuming and more effective. We'll cover this topic shortly.)

Remember, twenty or thirty years ago seeing lots of Japanese engineers traveling around the United States taking photographs? Care to guess what they were doing? In-context market research. The point here is that you don't need to have an established supplier-customer relationship in order to use this process. Bill Barnard recalls standing on a Tokyo street corner at 10:00 P.M., watching a Scottish engineer from NCR observing and taking notes about how the Japanese used a competitor's automated teller machine (ATM). NCR, incidentally, is the company that effectively drove IBM out of the ATM business and today is one of the largest ATM producers in Europe and Asia.[8] They understand that the essence of in-context market research is *observing the customers in their actual use of the product or service.*

Other companies doing an excellent job of conducting highly focused, structured visits include Raychem, Polaroid, CIGNA, Metropolitan Life, Milliken, and Du-Pont.[9]

Speaking of competitors, it's also a good idea to do in-context visits with your *potential* customers, i.e., the people who do business with other companies but not with you. Setting up these visits may take more effort, but normally they can be arranged without too much difficulty. Another fertile area consists of customers who also do substantial business with your competition. Who should make these visits? In general terms, the people responsible for making the product development decisions. In this way, the developers hear—first hand and unfiltered—what the customers are asking for. When the item being developed is a physical product, the in-context market research should be performed by members of the product development team. For strategy setting, the same principle applies: the in-context visits should be performed by the top management group, which is the development team for the Management Product.

Does this actually happen? Do executives actually make in-context visits? Absolutely. One example is John Young who, during his years as CEO at Hewlett-Packard, was in the field routinely. One of his frequent stops: Procter & Gamble. Did John go to P&G to sell them computers? No, although his presence no doubt helped the HP sales effort. When touring P&G plants, or visiting with Procter President John Pepper in his office, John Young didn't pull an order blank out of his briefcase. His primary purpose was to learn what this large, sophisticated computer user was presently doing, what its future needs were, and how HP might meet those needs. The intelligence gained during these and other visits became important input into HP's strategic plans and product development processes.

Text Analysis

Let's double back to the topic of reducing the voluminous amounts of data that can result from in-context visits. Computerized systems exist today that can help a great deal; they enable *qualitative* information—the voice of the customer, in his or her words—to be reduced, combined, and synthesized. Further, with computerization, this information can be analyzed and understood far more easily than in the past.

Questionnaires, most often, are like objective tests in school. They ask for quantifiable responses: yes or no, preference rankings 1 through *n*, and/or multiple-choice kinds of answers. They don't have the ability to address unspoken customer wants. As such, they can do a reasonable job in capturing *expressed* wants, but rarely capture the essence of the voice of the customer—the *exciting* benefits that are so important to determine in the competitive marketplace. Given enough questions on a questionnaire, it may be theoretically possible to arrive at some unspoken wants; however the customer won't be willing to answer hundreds of questions.

On the other hand, in-context customer visits—given the proper preparation, and with responses recorded, transcribed, and processed via computerized software—can yield the best of both worlds:

1. Customer responses are captured in their own voice, and that's critically important. The bad news is that these responses tend to be "soft," "fuzzy," "unfocused."
2. The power of the computer is used for data reduction, combination, synthesis, and reporting and the objectivity that only the computer can provide enhances the process.

Professor Hanan Polansky of the University of Rochester, a pioneer in this field, cites a number of important benefits here. One of them is that people express their attitudes much better in their natural language, rather than by means of a numerical scale. Another, Polansky says, is that the "computer does not develop 'filters,' regardless of the amount of text analyzed. The output is, therefore, an unbiased representation of the customer's attitudes. Moreover, *the novel ideas the customers suggest, the ones that point to untapped business opportunities, are captured.*" (Emphasis ours.)

> **MYTH: The customers don't know what they want today, much less in the future.**
>
> **FACT: Customers always know what benefits they want, but they can't always verbalize them. In-context customer visits, often coupled with text analysis software, can lead to breakthrough discoveries about what the customer wants.**

Many people always wanted a Sony Walkman; they just weren't aware of it. They became aware of this want only after seeing the product. Sony was able to "get inside the customers' environment" and extract this want from the random, varied, scattered comments of their customer base.

THE TOOLS IN ACTION:
In-Context Customer Research at Black & Decker

Black & Decker, the giant power tool manufacturer, perceived a niche in the marketplace: a void that could be
worth filling in the upper end of the do-it-yourself (DIY)
market. This is the mid-price segment—in between the
low-price, $35 per unit products and the pricey profes-
sional lines which are aimed at contractors and other professionals. The customers in this category, the "power
DIYers," tend to tackle major projects; they want more
capabilities than the standard tools offer; they are price-
sensitive; and their numbers have grown significantly over
the past few years.

To capture and to truly understand the voice of these
customers, Black & Decker developed a panel—a "living
laboratory" of fifty DIYers who owned more than six
power tools each. *Fortune* magazine reported: "From June
to September 1991 they were questioned about the tools
they used and why they had picked particular brands. B&D
marketing executives hung out with them in their homes
and around their workshops. They watched how the 50
used their tools and asked why they liked or disliked certain ones, how the tools felt in their hands, and even how
they cleaned up their work space when they were finished.
The B&D people tagged along on shopping trips too, mon-
itoring what the DIYers bought and how much they
spent."[10]

This plus other research convinced the Black & Decker
executives that they could give these customers everything
they wanted, and more. The product: the Quantum line of
power tools. This does not consist solely of the tools themselves; the "total product" also includes free maintenance
checks at B&D service centers and a toll-free hotline staffed

by experienced advisers to answer questions. CEO Nolan Archibald says: "The whole point behind this product line was to have it driven to market by what the consumers really wanted."

Financial analyst Susan Gallagher, who tracks this industry closely, estimates that the Quantum product line will generate between $30 and $40 million in sales in a little over its first year of existence. "Black & Decker has become very good at taking market share away from rival companies," she says. "They just know their customers."

So far, we've looked at tools for idea generation: focus groups and in-context visits. Now let's examine a breakthrough tool for idea testing.

CHOICE MODELING[11]

Choice Modeling is a system for finding out which attributes—or characteristics—of a product or service should be provided to customers to increase the probability that they will buy. The word "attribute" is used very broadly. It encompasses

- features and attributes of the product itself
- how well the product works
- how the product is packaged
- how the product is invoiced
- how the product is serviced
- how readily available the product is
- how "tailorable" the product is
- how the product is priced

The customer's decision-making process is quantified, and a separate "predictive model of choice" is created for each individual customer, using that person's values and perceptions.

Choice Modeling, using questionnaires, asks the customer to assign importance weights to various product/service characteristics (sometimes called the "desire profile"). The desire profile represents a comprehensive description of which characteristics people want in the product/service, and also *the extent to which they want each one* of these characteristics—how much value they place on each feature.

Then the customers indicate the characteristics they believe describe not only the company's existing products/services but also those of the competitors. The resulting data base can provide valuable descriptive information:

- do the customers want a given characteristic;
- how intensely do they want it, compared to all the other characteristics being studied;
- do the customers believe that existing products/services have that characteristic; and
- to what extent do customers attribute different characteristics to the various products currently available, both our own products and those of the competition?

Larry Gibson of Eric Marder Associates, a leading developer of Choice Modeling technology,[12] maintains that "conventional analysis does not even scratch the surface of the real problem. This is because conventional analysis depends on 'averaging' data in one way or another—a manner of handling data that simply does not correspond to how the world is made.

"Products are bought by *individuals*, not by groups, and each individual has unique desires and unique beliefs. The central problem the marketer faces is that he is offering *one* product to *many* people. And the central problem the analyst faces is to find out which *one* offer will most effectively attract *many* buyers. Almost by definition, this cannot be done by averaging." Larry goes on to say that surveys typically produce descriptions (e.g., of the "average" customer); what's needed are *predictions* of what they'll buy and from whom.

Choice Modeling, therefore, makes it possible to take the diversity of desires and beliefs into account without artificial averaging.

Let's revisit our author's computer purchase. Choice-based research would have asked him to assign weightings to grade the importance of the various characteristics of his ideal computer. He would have responded as shown in Figure 2-1. We refer to this as the $100 test. It asks the question: If you had $100 to spend to help get what you want among all these factors, how would you spend that money? How would you allocate the $100?

One of his possible choices, Computer A, is a fine ma-

FIGURE 2-1: The $100 Test

CHARACTERISTIC	IMPORTANCE
High Speed (486/33)	$ 5 (or %)
Large Disk (120MB)	5
Good Screen	20
Color Screen	5
Battery Life (>2 HRS)	5
Weight (<6 Pounds)	30
Full Function Keyboard	25
Built-in Modem	2
Built-in Trackball or Mouse	1
Docking Station	2
	$100 (or %)

chine: fast, large storage, long battery life. He didn't buy that one. He bought Computer B: an older machine, slower, with a smaller disk and shorter battery life—for only a bit less money than A. Why? See Figure 2-2 for his choice preferences.

In this one *isolated* example, the customer preferred a technologically inferior product by a margin of almost 2 to 1. Computer A had twice as many "yes" features (8) as B (4). However, Computer B matched the buyer's choice preference far better, outscoring Computer A by 77 to 44. Major factors affecting the customer's decision were his highly valued characteristics of screen (20%), weight (30%), and keyboard (25%).

Think of a data base containing the importance ratings from thousands of individuals, along with the characteristics of each individual. It then becomes a practical matter to

FIGURE 2-2: The $100 Test Applied to a Computer Purchase

CHARACTERISTIC	IMPORTANCE	COMPUTER A		B	
High Speed (486/33)	$ 5 (or %)	YES:	5 PTS	NO	
Large Disk (120MB)	5	Y	5	N	
Good Screen	20	Y	20	Y	20
Color Screen	5	Y	5	N	
Battery Life (>2 HRS)	5	Y	5	N	
Weight (<6 POUNDS)	30	N		Y	30
Full Function Keyboard	25	N		Y	25
Built-in Modem	2	Y	2	Y	2
Built-in Trackball or Mouse	1	Y	1	N	
Docking Station	2	Y	1	N	
Number of Yes Responses	$100 (or %)	44 PTS		77 PTS	
The Product Purchased Was:				B	

determine—for each person in the data base—whether they would buy Product A or Product B, C, or D, based on their choice preferences. These individual decisions can then be grouped by category of customer (demographics, geographics, occupation, etc.) or for the market as a whole.

Given that type of data base, it becomes a practical matter to *simulate* the effects of changes in our product versus the competition (or vice versa). The computer determines, for each customer, whether the proposed change would make enough of a difference for them to change their buying preference. In other words, has the higher perceived value (benefits vs. price) shifted from one product to another?

"What-if" analysis—simulation—is the essence of Choice Modeling. Here are a few possible questions that would be readily answered by a good choice model:

- What changes in market share would occur as a result of which changes to our product?
- What if a competitor lowers its price by 20%, what's the effect on our market share?
- Which array of features in the new product would capture the greatest market share in a given category of customer?
- If we add a certain feature to the product and thus have to increase its price, how much market share would we gain and how much would we lose—and in what customer categories?

The possibilities are endless.

THE TOOLS IN ACTION:
Choice Modeling at the Ford Foundation

A few years ago, the Ford Foundation undertook a major project—The Finances of the Performing Arts—in response to significant funding problems for the arts. Along with collecting financial data, the Foundation also commissioned a market research study of the audiences for these classic performing arts—including symphony, opera, and ballet—using Choice Modeling.[13]

One course of action which had been discussed was to change the public's perception of customary and acceptable dress—to move it down market—on the premise that more people would attend concerts and performances if such functions weren't perceived as "dressy." After all, the reasoning went, dress habits are much more casual now, and many more people might attend if they could do so in bluejeans and sweaters.

On the surface, there seemed to be solid support for this theory. The belief that "dressiness" is expected at the arts is widely held and, at least on the average, is in fact a deterrent to attending. However, when choice model simulations of this strategy were made and analyzed one-person-at-a-time, it was learned that this approach would literally hurt attendance. The following simulations showed the explanation for this apparent contradiction:

1. Many people who believe the performing arts are too dressy would not attend them under any circumstances. So, *their opinions on the dress code are irrelevant.*
2. Many others who believe that the arts are too dressy are, at the same time, passionate devotees. They attend frequently, but they disregard the dressiness factor. They're the ones up in the third balcony, wearing bluejeans and sweaters. They will attend under any circum-

stances, and so *their opinions on dress are also irrelevant.*

3. Some people don't like the performing arts enough to get dressed up for them. But, if they were less dressy, *they might come.*
4. Some people attend these performances just because they *are* dressy events. They enjoy seeing and being seen. They may also enjoy the performance, but it's somewhat secondary. If the arts are made less dressy, *they will stop coming.*

People in categories 3 and 4 are said to be in the "*cusp of choice.*" They are the people who might become customers given some changes (category 3), or customers who are held narrowly but could be lost (category 4). The cusp of choice is where the battle for increased attendance—or increased market share—will be won or lost.

For the performing arts, the Ford Foundation study found there were *fewer people in category 3 than in 4.* Thus, lowering the implicit dress code would cause attendance to *decrease*, not increase. The choice model pegged the estimated audience loss at 8 percent for ballet, 5 percent for symphony, and 3 percent for opera.

Had the boards of trustees of performing arts organizations followed their instincts, they would have changed their marketing approach—how they present their "product" to the public—by lowering the implicit dress code. This would have been a major strategic error, one that was avoided through the use of choice modeling.

MYTH: The marketplace is simply too diffuse, too diverse, too complex, and too unpredictable to get your arms around.

FACT: The customer knowledge gained during in-context visits and the logic of choice modeling—

coupled with the power of the computer—enables insights into the marketplace not possible until recently.

These are important elements of the top management's new set of tools. They help the executive group to develop its Management Product effectively, with high quality, and with an intense customer focus. Bill BonDurant points out that these kinds of processes have had "a profound bottom-line impact on the way Hewlett-Packard addresses the marketplace."

SUCCESS FACTORS:
DOs and DON'Ts

DON'T skimp on the resources—time and money—required for effective market research.

DON'T delegate the in-context visits to others in the company or to outsiders. The top management team needs to conduct these visits themselves. They will produce the Management Product, and thus they need to have first-hand input from the customers.

DO get training on these new market research approaches and, if necessary, on interviewing skills so that the in-context visits can be conducted in a structured, effective manner.

DO make sure you visit a good cross-section of customers, not just the ones with whom you're on very good terms.

Market research expert Edward McQuarrie points out that "It is difficult to discover new things if you always visit a small coterie of favorite customers. . . . A particularly subtle trap comes about through concentrating one's visits on so-called national accounts, A-list customers, or very large customers. The rationale, of course, is that these people account for a substantial fraction of your sales. But why is this so? Might there also be large users who are small customers of yours (because your product is not quite right for them)? If so, then the most rapid expansion of sales might come from visiting and learning about customers who are not buying very much from you today."[14]

It's time to check with the folks at B&W and get their reactions to these market research opportunities.

Four days later, at the B&W executive staff meeting, VP of Marketing Mike Perez presented his thoughts on some new approaches to market research. A heated discussion on benefits and costs—in terms of both dollars and people's time— followed. After a while, CEO Charles Evans said: "I think we've kicked this around enough. I'd like to get a reaction from each of you as to what we should do." Turning to his immediate right, he said: "Fran, how about if you start off?"

Fran Collier, VP Finance: "I like what Mike had to say. I like it a lot. I recommend we do it. The question I have is, What is it? In other words, how much market research should we do here at the outset—a little bit, a whole lot, or something in the middle? Which of these market research tools should we use? I'm most intrigued by what Mike said about in-context customer visits. I think it would really be good for all of us to get involved in that kind of process. Harry?"

"Yeah, that makes sense to me," said Harold Simon, VP Human Resources. "But I think we'll need some training in interviewing skills and techniques. I have a feeling there may be more to this than meets the eye."

Paul Lewis, VP Product Development, commented, "You know, I haven't verbalized this yet, but my gut has been telling me for some time that we're deficient in customer knowledge. But it's not just the end users of the products that we need to look at; we've got to cover the entire value chain—the wholesalers, the retailers, school systems, businesses, other institutions. We need to get eyeball-to-eyeball with all those kinds of folks. So it sounds as though we're on the right track. But I've got a question for you, Charlie: Once we get all this wonderful customer feedback, what the hell are we going to do with it?"

"It's simple, Paul. We're going to reset the strategic direction of this company. Since Mike brought this topic up last week," Charlie Evans went on, "I've read some of the material he gave me, and I've given it a lot of thought. If we learn only half as much as I think we will, I'll be amazed if we don't wind up doing a major recalibration of our strategic plans. But don't let me bias the discussion. Owen, what do you think?"

Owen Barnes, VP Operations: "Shoot, let's do the whole deal. Why stop with just the in-context visits? Why don't we run some focus groups? Why not do that exotic stuff—what d'ya call it, Paul?—Choice Modeling, too? I'm for pulling out all the stops. Let's crank it up. We need to grow the top line. Don't you agree, Mike?"

"Owen, my heart agrees with you; I'm really pumped up about this. But my head says that we should walk before we run," Mike Perez responded. "I like Fran's idea of starting with in-context visits. That should give us enough to do what Charlie just said—set the overall strategies. Then as we get into more specific stuff—like product design, how we service our wholesalers, and so on—we can do the Choice Modeling if that makes sense to us at the time, as I believe it will.

"Even before we do the in-context visits, though, we should consider holding a few focus groups—on a purely blue-sky, idea generation basis. This'll help us develop the format and

questions for the customer visits. Up until now, we've been using focus groups for idea testing—'How do you like this pencil'—rather than for idea generation, which might ask: 'How do you use a writing implement in your day-to-day activities, and how could it be made easier or better for you?'

Mike continued, "You've all met Brenda Kelly, our new business planning manager? Well, Brenda was appalled when she saw some of the market research we've done. She's only been on board a short time, but she's really the one who got me started down this path. Anyway, are you okay, Owen?"

"You bet."

"If we do this in-context research," Charles Evans said, "I really think we need to do it ourselves. We shouldn't farm it out and we shouldn't delegate it. What this means, folks, is that each one of us is signing up for some extra work and some extra travel. Are you game?"

Paul (Product Development): "Yes sir. And I agree with Harry that we'll need some front-end training."

Harry (Human Resources): "Count me in. I spent some of the happiest years of my life calling on customers."

Owen (Operations): "When do we start?"

Mike (Marketing): "Could I possibly say no?"

Fran (Finance): "I'm game. But I do have one more question: After we capture all this voice of the customer data and get it put together, exactly how are we going to get it into our strategic plans?"

Silence.

Then Mike Perez grinned and said, "At that seminar I went to we learned about a new technique that started out as a product development tool, but lately it's being used to set strategies. Maybe we should take a look at it—it's called QFD."

CHAPTER 3

Linking Customers
to Strategy

In mid-April Michael Perez, B&W's Vice President of Marketing, was speaking to the company's executive group at a meeting. "Ladies and gentlemen, I'd like to recap what's happened on the new strategy project over the past ninety days—just to make sure we're all on the same page—and then get into the results of the in-context customer visits that you all so diligently participated in.

"First, we felt we needed to call this activity something, so we've given it a name: Project Innovation.

"Second, shortly after the January meeting when we decided to do this, we asked Brenda Kelly to join the project team. Our reasons were that Brenda's job as business planning manager is deeply involved with strategic planning—which is the focus of this project—and also that she has hands-on market research experience from her ten years at General Mills. She's been quarterbacking the market research phase of this project, so at this point I'd like to turn the meeting over to Brenda."

"Thanks, Mike. Well, folks, I can tell you it's been a labor of love. I'm convinced we're on the right track with what we're doing here.

"I'd like to continue with Mike's recap. The third thing we did, at my recommendation, was to pull in an outside firm to help us with the market research and some of the subsequent phases of the project. Even though I've been through some of this process—specifically, the market research—I haven't personally been involved in the subsequent steps and, believe me, they're critical. As you know, the consultants conducted our initial training and helped with the design of the questions for the in-context visits. As the process continues, they'll be in at specified times throughout the project.

"Fourth, we did the in-context customer visits over the last six weeks or so. I compiled a list of the different kinds of customers we visited with, and it looks pretty impressive:

- *businesses*
- *universities*
- *hospitals*
- *other nonprofit agencies*
- *professional and business people on airplanes and in airline club rooms*
- *office supply dealers*
- *office supply distributors*
- *major discounters*

"In total, we did twenty-seven in-context sessions, which works out to an average of about four visits for each of us. This is particularly impressive when one considers that, in a given customer visit, we might have talked to three or more different "customers," i.e., decision makers, not just the end users. I think it's great that you folks put your time and effort into this. We're doing it right, and it's exciting.

"Fifth, we've transcribed all of the tapes. Incidentally, I can get you either hard copy or a diskette of any or all of the

transcripts if you'd like to have them. However, you might not find it necessary, thanks to the next point.

"Sixth, we used an outside text analysis firm to do the data reduction and to search for patterns or clusters in the responses. Their software runs on a big mainframe; however, they've provided us with a data base that is usable on our PCs. With that, Mike and I have been working interactively with the condensed, synthesized responses coming out of our in-context visits. I'd be delighted to give you a demo on this, either individually or as a group."

Fran: "What's the cost of that service, Brenda?"

"I don't have their final bill yet, but it'll be between thirty-five and forty thousand. But, you know, it's actually more of an investment than a cost. We'll be able to keep this data for future use. I'd like to see it become part of a comprehensive customer data base that we maintain over the long run. Okay?"

"Right."

"Let's see what we've got. What are these results telling us? Well, they're telling us a lot of things, but perhaps the most important is that we may have identified a major opportunity in the market, a customer want that is currently going unfilled. The research data shows a degree of frustration with having to use multiple tools: a ballpoint pen, a pencil, an erasable pen, red ink, blue lead, a highlighter, etc. This want is coming primarily from people who travel a lot and from people who write a great deal: reporters, academics, authors, technical folks, and—perhaps surprisingly—students. A secondary factor here seems to be a desire not to look like a nerd—with a bunch of pens and pencils sticking out of a plastic pocket protector.

"Also reinforcing this may be a societal shift away from

'luxury' products into products with a high degree of utility and practicality. If the 1980s were the decade of expensive German sedans—forgive me, Charlie—then the 1990s might turn out to be the decade of domestic minivans. The upper end of the pen and pencil market is not good; rumors have it that Cross, Waterman, Montblanc, et al., are struggling.

"Here's a list of the top six end-user customer wants as uncovered by our in-context visits:

- *fewer pens and pencils to carry around*
- *serve a variety of purposes*
- *makes my writing look good*
- *easy to use*
- *looks good in my pocket*
- *easy to get refills*

"As far as our intermediate customers are concerned—the wholesalers and retailers—here are their top six wants:

- *better availability of product (no back orders)*
- *better availability of information (from our internal Customer Service Department and our field sales force)*
- *no split shipments*
- *more profitable products*
- *more exciting products*
- *no invoicing errors."*

*A*t this point, B&W Inc. is well into the discovery process. They've done a good job of capturing and understanding the voice of the customer. Now, in very general terms, let's preview what the top management team will have to do next:

1. Rank the customer *wants* according to their preferences, as expressed in the $100 test.

2. Evaluate how the competition is doing in meeting these *wants.*

3. Determine how the company can meet the customer *wants.* These are called *"hows."*

4. Assign target values for each *how.* An example of a target value for a pizza home delivery service might be 30 minutes or less. A *how* with a target value is called a *"measure."*

5. Evaluate the degree to which each *measure* will support each *want.*

6. Assess how well the competition is meeting the *measures.* Search for areas of competitor weakness that can be exploited.

7. Identify trade-offs among the *measures.*

8. Look for breakthrough opportunities, ones which can have high impact on the competitive position of the business.

Let's start with the *wants* from the end users. What these people are telling B&W is summarized in Figure 3-1.

FIGURE 3-1: Customer *Wants*

Superior Writing Instrument
Fewer pens/pencils to carry
Serves a variety of purposes
Makes writing look good
Easy to use
Looks good
Easy to get refills

(*Note:* the figures in this and the next chapter will sometimes lead the reader to rotate the page 90 degrees in order to read the vertical text and numbers more easily. The output from QFD software looks like this, reflecting one of the basic features of the QFD matrix process: to see the relationship of elements at right angles to each other.)

CUSTOMER PREFERENCES

During the market research phase, it's necessary to capture how the customers feel about the *relative* importance of each of the attributes. Let's assume that the B&W people used the $100 test (see Chapter 2) during their in-context visits. In Figure 3-2, we can see the results of that. The customers assigned 25 dollars and 35 dollars respectively to the first two *wants*, representing 60 percent of the total importance.

Note the attribute of "Makes [my] writing look good"

FIGURE 3-2: Ranked Customer *Wants*

	Customer Importance — $100 test	Ranked Order of Importance
Superior Writing Instrument		
Fewer pens/pencils to carry	25	2
Serves a variety of purposes	35	1
Makes writing look good		
Easy to use	20	3
Looks good	5	5
Easy to get refills	15	4

with no value to the right of it. Even though the customers identified this as a *want*, it received little emphasis in the $100 test (probably averaging less than $1). Even though the customers said they wanted it, the $100 test showed that it was a very low purchase priority for them.

EVALUATE THE COMPETITION

Thus far, we've talked a lot about customers and the central role they must play. However, competitors are another major factor impacting on how companies develop and execute their strategic plan. A strategy developed in a competitive vacuum—not taking the competition into account—would not be worth the paper on which it's written.

Can QFD help in evaluating the competition? Indeed it can. In Figure 3-3, from left to right, we can see how QFD presents competitor-related information:

- customer *wants*;
- results of the $100 test (column 1) and how these results rank (column 2);
- a graph showing how the identified competitors stack up (column 3); and
- in columns 4 through 6, the competitors' weighted scores on a scale of 1 (low) to 5 (high).

This example shows three competitors being evaluated: the Pentel Multi-Instrument (containing eight writing tools); the Fisher Four Pen (with three inks and one lead); and the Platinum Pen (same as the Fisher but much more attractive). If B&W already had a product in this category, its customer perception data would also be shown here.

The maximum score is a 5; the minimum value a 1. Let's

FIGURE 3-3: Customer's Perception of the Competition

Superior Writing Instrument	Customer Importance — $100 Test	Ranked Order of Importance	Maximum Value = 5.0 / • — Pentel Multi-Instr / □ — Fisher Four Pen / ★ — Platinum Pen / Minimum Value = 1.0	Pentel Multi-Instr	Fisher Four Pen	Platinum Pen
Fewer pens/pencils to carry	25	2		5	3	4
Serves a variety of purposes	35	1		5	3	4
Makes writing look good				4	3	3
Easy to use	20	3		1	2	2
Looks good	5	5		3	2	5
Easy to get refills	15	4		1	2	2

examine how the Pentel was evaluated: it scored 5 on the customer *wants* of fewer pens/pencils to carry around and on serves a variety of purposes. This stands to reason, because it contains three pens and five leads. However, the Pentel was rated very low on easy to use and on easy to get refills.

Please note that the other two competitive products also scored poorly on these same two customer *wants*. This is potentially a significant piece of information to the B&W team—even though these *wants* ranked only third and fourth respectively. A major product benefit, and thus a source of differentiation and competitive advantage, might be achieved here.

B&W could decide to make a major effort at making its product very simple to use and refills very easy to get, because the competitors are doing a poor job. This is another example of a discovery—a breakthrough insight— that results from the intelligent use of QFD.

IDENTIFY THE *HOWS*

Let's assume that, at the mid-April meeting, the B&W folks did the brainstorming and developed the following array of *hows*:

> number of colors of ink
> number of types of lead
> proper shape, size, and weight
> erasure capability
> instructions easy to understand quickly
> up-market, hi-tech appearance
> refills readily available

At this point, B&W's Project Innovation team—the executive group plus Brenda Kelly plus the outside facilitator—can begin to construct its first QFD chart, which we'll call the Phase I House. See Figure 3-4.

ASSIGN TARGET VALUES

Next, the team researched and assigned "target values" to each of the *hows*. Wherever possible, target values are expressed in quantified terms. They've been added to the diagram shown in Figure 3-5.

Hows plus target values equal measures. These *measures*,

FIGURE 3-4: _Wants_ vs. _Hows_

	Number of colors of ink	Number of types of leads	Size, shape, weight	Eraser capability	Quick easy instructions	Hi-tech look	Ease of acquiring refills
Superior Writing Instrument							
Fewer pens/pencils to carry							
Serves a variety of purposes							
Makes writing look good							
Easy to use							
Looks good							
Easy to get refills							

which will be used early in the QFD process, are very general. They do not refer to the _specifics_ of how the company will meet the customers wants. Rather, they refer to what the company can measure and control that will provide delight. Subsequently, some of these _measures_ will become _wants;_ they will drive the development of more specific _hows_ which will direct the company's strategic plans.

Note that the _hows_ are at right angles to the _wants._ Further, the target values are lined up directly below their respective _hows._ This arrangement facilitates the next step.

FIGURE 3-5: *Hows* with Target Values

	Number of colors of ink	Number of types of leads	Size, shape, weight	Eraser capability	Quick easy instructions	Hi-tech look	Ease of acquiring refills
Superior Writing Instrument							
Fewer pens/pencils to carry							
Serves a variety of purposes							
Makes writing look good							
Easy to use							
Looks good							
Easy to get refills							
	3 or more - R, B, BLK	3 or more - Ld, Rd, Ylw	= or < Montblanc	Lead, Ink	<5 min to use	Do Studies	< 24 hrs

SET THE RELATIONSHIPS

Next, the team needs to establish the relationships between *wants* and *hows*. For every *want*, it will ask: Does each *how* support this *want* and, if so, to what extent does it support it? Is the relationship between this *want* and this *how* strong, medium, weak, or nonexistent?

Symbols are used for this weighting:

Strong relationship	●
Moderate relationship	○
Weak relationship	△

After establishing the relationships between all of the *wants* and all of the *hows*, the B&W team's QFD House might appear as shown in Figure 3-6.

Now let's add the customer importance factors ($100 test) into the QFD House (Figure 3-7).

Another general practice within QFD concerns the impact—the relative weighting—assigned to the relationships. A moderate relationship is considered to be three times more important than a weak one, and a strong relationship three times more important than one that's moderate. There's nothing magic about these numbers; some companies have used others. But, over the years, the 1–3–9 relationship has proven to yield quantitative results which make sense and match the users subjective, qualitative viewpoints. Therefore:

WEIGHTING

Strong relationship	●	9
Moderate relationship	○	3
Weak relationship	△	1

FIGURE 3-6: Relationships Between *Wants* and *Hows*

WANTS vs. MEASURES Legend	Number of colors of ink	Number of types of leads	Size, shape, weight	Eraser capability	Quick easy instructions	Hi-tech look	Ease of acquiring refills
Strong ● 9 / Moderate ○ 3 / Weak △ 1							
Superior Writing Instrument							
Fewer pens/pencils to carry	●	●				△	
Serves a variety of purposes	●	●		△		△	
Makes writing look good			●	○			
Easy to use			●	○	○		
Looks good		○				●	
Easy to get refills							●
	3 or more - R, B, BLK	3 or more - Ld, Rd, Ylw	= or < Montblanc	Lead, Ink	<5 min to use	Do Studies	< 24 hrs

FIGURE 3-7: Relationships with $100 Test

WANTS vs. MEASURES Legend		Number of colors of ink	Number of types of leads	Size, shape, weight	Eraser capability	Quick easy instructions	Hi-tech look	Ease of acquiring refills	Customer Importance — $100 Test	Ranked Order of Importance
Strong ● 9										
Moderate ○ 3										
Weak △ 1										
Superior Writing Instrument										
Fewer pens/pencils to carry		●	●					△	25	2
Serves a variety of purposes		●	●		△			△	35	1
Makes writing look good				●	○					
Easy to use				●	○	○			20	3
Looks good				○			●		5	5
Easy to get refills								●	15	4

The ● at the intersection of the first *want* (fewer pens/ pencils) and the first *how* (multiple pens) has a raw value of 9. When applied to the customer importance factor of 25 (the outcome of the $100 test for fewer pens/pencils), it has a weighted value of $9 \times 25 = 225$. See Figure 3-8 for these calculated values and the totals.

At this point, a disclaimer might be in order: it's not necessary to do all of these calculations manually. Software exists to do all of this and more. It runs on personal computers; it's easy to use; and it's not expensive. (See Appendix A for details.)

FIGURE 3-8: *Hows* Weighted and Ranked

Superior Writing Instrument	Number of colors of ink	Number of types of leads	Size, shape, weight	Eraser capability	Quick, easy instructions	Hi-tech look	Ease of aquiring refills	Customer Importance — $100 Test	Ranked Order of Importance
Fewer pens/pencils to carry	9	9				1		25	2
Serves a variety of purposes	9	9		1		1		35	1
Makes writing look good			9	3					
Easy to use			9	3	3			20	3
Looks good			3			9		5	5
Easy to get refills							9	15	4
Weighted Value	540	540	195	95	60	105	135	1	2
Ranked Value	1	1	3	6	7	5	4		
	3 or more - R, B, BLK	3 or more - Ld, Rd, Ylw	= or < Montblanc	Lead, Ink	<5 min to use	Do Studies	< 24 hrs		

A more complete QFD House is shown in Figure 3-9, containing several new pieces of information, one at the bottom of the diagram below the target values, and one at the top above the *hows*.

ADDITIONAL COMPETITIVE INFORMATION

Let's first look at the information shown below the target values. This contains the *company's* evaluation of how well the competition is doing in meeting the target values. (How the customers feel about the competition meeting their *wants* is shown in the upper-right portion of the QFD House, as we saw earlier.)

In our example, this competitive data versus the target values could strongly reinforce the possibility of significant marketplace potential for ease of use and easy to get refills. This becomes apparent when one looks at how the competition is doing against two measures:

1. Easy to use—understand it in less than 5 minutes: two competitors are rated mediocre and one poor.

2. Easy to get refills—less than 24 hours: all three competitors are rated poor.

Identify Trade-Offs

QFD can help to identify potential conflicts between two or more *hows*. These possible trade-offs can be identified in the peaked area at the top of the house, sometimes referred to as the "roof." (This is why the QFD matrix is referred to as a "house.")

Going back to Figure 3-9, we can see that a potential trade-off exists between the *how* of multiple pens and the *how* of size-shape-weight. It's the same for the *how* of multi-

FIGURE 3-9: The "House of Quality"

	Number of colors of ink	Number of types of leads	Size, shape, weight	Eraser capability	Quick, easy instructions	Hi-tech look	Ease of acquiring refills	Customer Importance — $100 Test	Ranked Order of Importance	Maximum Value = 5.0 / • — Pentel Multi-Instr / □ — Fisher Four Pen / * — Platinum Pen / Minimum Value = 1.0	Pentel Multi-Instr	Fisher Four Pen	Platinum Pen
Fewer pens/pencils to carry	•	•			Δ			25	2		5	3	4
Serves a variety of purposes	•	•	Δ		Δ			35	1		5	2	4
Makes writing look good			•	O							4	3	3
Easy to use			•	O	O			20	3		1	2	2
Looks good				O		•		5	5		3	2	5
Easy to get refills							•	15	4		1	2	2
Weighted Value	540	540	195	95	60	105	135						
Ranked Value	1	1	3	6	7	5	4						
Target Value of the Measure	3 or more - R, B, BLK	3 or more - Ld, Rd, Ylw	= or < Montblanc	Lead, Ink	<5 min to use	Do Studies	<24 hrs						

Maximum Value = 5.0
• — Pentel Multi-Instr
□ — Fisher Four Pen-B,R
*— Platinum Pen 3 Pn,1
Minimum Value = 1.0

	Number of colors of ink	Number of types of leads	Size, shape, weight	Eraser capability	Quick, easy instructions	Hi-tech look	Ease of acquiring refills
Pentel Multi-Instr	5	5	4		3	4	
Fisher Four Pen-B,R,G,Blk	3	1	1		3	2	2
Platinum Pen 3 Pn, 1 Ld	4	3	3	2	2	4	2

ple leads against size-shape-weight. In other words, the more pens and pencils that we have to stuff into this thing, the harder it's going to be to hit the targets for size, shape and weight. (Note: for clarity, we've left most of the "roof" blank. There are other negative correlations, plus some positive ones, which we haven't shown in Figure 3-9.)

Let's recap. In this chapter we've seen how the QFD House is constructed. The cross-functional QFD team—in our example, the B&W executive group—does the following:

1. Translates customer *wants* into *hows*, the measures by which the customers will know that their wants are being satisfied.
2. Assigns target values for each *how*, to create the measure.
3. Establishes relationships between each *how* and each *want*: strong, moderate, weak, or none. In this step, synergy is often identified: a given *how*, created to meet a certain *want*, may have positive effects on other *wants*. The QFD process helps to identify those synergistic relationships, and to quantify them. (We'll see more of this in the next chapter.)
4. Applies customer importance factors and competitive evaluations.
5. Identifies trade-offs between *hows*. This is done in the correlation matrix, the "roof of the house"; it helps to focus on the *hows* that are in conflict.
6. Analyzes the information in the QFD House, makes decisions based on this information, and identifies the primary inputs into their Management Product, i.e., the company's strategic plans.

Note the robustness of the QFD House. The intent here is to get all of the relevant information onto a single piece of paper. (In actual practice, good QFD software enables this display to be magnified several times to make it more readable.)

MYTH: It's impossible to deal with more than a few variables at a time.

FACT: Existing information, recombined and arranged in innovative ways, enables people to "see through" the complexity and often leads to breakthrough discoveries.

QFD gets all of the relevant information—customer *wants* and importance ratings, the company's potential responses, competitive factors, etc.—onto one piece of paper. It's then possible to perceive the interplay between a number of variables, and this frequently results in "lights going on." "Aha!," "Wow!" and "Look at that!" are frequently heard in QFD sessions. These kinds of insights dramatically increase the quality of the Management Product.

THE TOOLS IN ACTION:
Business Strategy Development via QFD at
Pierce & Stevens

Pierce & Stevens is a Buffalo-based manufacturer of high-quality adhesives, sold primarily to producers of food products and other consumer package goods. An old-line company, it employs several hundred people and is a division of Pratt & Lambert, a major player in the paint industry. Continuity of employment at Pierce & Stevens is very strong throughout the company; among the top five executives, for example, the average length of employment with the company is over twenty years, and they know the business very well.

Pierce & Stevens has closely followed the processes outlined in this book. All of the steps listed below were performed by the executive team, consisting of the president and the vice presidents of Finance, Marketing, Operations and Sales, and R&D. This activity took place in the third quarter of 1993, as a part of the annual planning cycle.

1. Customer information—wants, needs, problem-solving opportunities—was gathered diligently. The $100 test was included in this process.
2. The customer *wants* were grouped and *hows* were developed.
3. The QFD House was constructed, and values—strong, medium, weak, or nonexistent—were assigned to each of the several hundred relationships.
4. Weightings from the $100 test were applied to each of the assigned values, totals were calculated, and the *hows* were ranked by potential. Computer software did this number crunching.

The results: two *significant discoveries* were uncovered, with breakthrough potential. They are expected to *dramatically alter* the relationship between Pierce & Stevens and its customers, and to provide *substantial differentiation* from the competition.

Dave Peacock, Vice President of Marketing, says: "Using QFD, we made more progress with strategic planning in a few days than we did in dozens of days over the past eight years." His enthusiasm is shared by the other four members of the executive team, including Vice President of Operations & Sales John Edholm, who stated: "As we finished presenting our strategic plan to Corporate, we got a round of applause. I've been with this company for over twenty years, and I can guarantee you that doesn't happen very often."

The breakthroughs discovered in the strategic planning/

QFD process have led to five specific action plans, which are being implemented as we write this in the fourth quarter of 1993.

SUCCESS FACTORS:
DOs and DON'Ts

DO make certain that your customer *wants* are truly that—and not merely what some people in the company think the customers want. The need for solid customer information is absolute; it will directly affect the quality of everything else that occurs in the process. Garbage in garbage out.

DON'T try to use QFD without training. Mark Bailey, one of Hewlett-Packard's highly experienced QFD users, says: "One essential for successful QFD is support and training."

DON'T try to do this without expert facilitation. Here's Mark Bailey again: "Another essential for successful QFD is expert facilitation, by a person who is not part of the organization doing the QFD process." Mark goes on to point out that, left to our own devices, we pay more and more attention to things of less and less importance to our customers. It's essential to have an uninvolved person—QFD knowledgeable—who can help the group through the process, serve as a coach and an arbitrator, and maintain focus on the customer.

The early results of B&W's new *Project Innovation team* were discussed at a later meeting.
Brenda Kelly wrapped up: "So what we have here is a very strong set of customer wants *which is leading us to a totally*

different product—one that might be called a multi-functional writing instrument."

"Isn't this fascinating!" said Paul Lewis. "It's like looking through a microscope; we can see things that weren't visible before."

Fran Collier: "Yeah, it's exciting. And it's scary. If we do this, it's going to cost an arm and a leg. I'm glad we're sitting on a bunch of cash."

Charles Evans glanced at his VP of Operations. "Owen, do I remember you saying your group was looking for a challenge? Looks like your wish may come true."

"Me and my big mouth," said Owen Barnes smiling. "This is a challenge and a half. Charlie, we've never done anything like this before. Not even close. Unless I miss my guess, it's going to call for tighter tolerances and a higher precision in manufacturing than we've ever done before."

"Can you do it?"

"I won't know until we see more of what it looks like. But I'll say this: if it's doable, we can do it. I believe our manufacturing capabilities are as good as any in the industry—and that includes Japan and Europe. Paul, can you design it so that we can build it?"

Paul: "Same answer as yours, Owen—I don't know. But I do know that we can't design it on our own. We'll have to have a multi-functional team, with strong representation from your manufacturing people. Remember, we did concurrent design with the new rollerball we launched last year. It went great. The only problem was that the customers weren't as impressed as we were—they haven't bought many."

"Don't remind me," replied Mike. "But back to the present. From a marketing perspective, I can envision a whole line of multi-function writing instruments like this. We may start with just one product, but I can see it evolving into much more. In other words, the product line would have multiple products, and each product would have multiple writing tools."

Charlie: "Mike, I like that a lot. We need a breakthrough strategy to get us out of the rut we're in. And we are in a rut, in our own minds as well as the public's. This totally different family of products may be just the ticket. We'll probably want to launch with one product only, but be able to expand the line quickly."

"Here's a name for it—OmniPen," said Harry Simon enthusiastically. "I can see the ad copy now: 'The OmniPen line from B&W—writing implements for the twenty-first century.'"

"Harry, that great," Charlie responded, "but I'm afraid we may be running away with this thing. Which is fine, I suppose. We haven't had this much energy at one of our meetings in a long time. But, as Fran said, this is potentially very big. We've got a ton of homework to do just to get some preliminary financial numbers.

"There's a board of directors' meeting in about five weeks. By the end of the month, I'd like for us to make a preliminary decision as whether or not to present this. All right?"

Nods of assent from all present.

Then Mike spoke up again. "I think we're all agreed that this is an 800-pound gorilla. It's bigger than anything we've ever done. If we go ahead with it, how in the world are we going to make sure we've got this thing coordinated and that we don't lose our focus on the customer?"

Brenda Kelly responded, "Mike, I think QFD can help us here also. We can take the measures—the hows plus the target values—from this first house, and pass them along as wants to *teams in Marketing, Operations, and Product Development. They'll use them, and the QFD matrix process, to develop the marketing strategy, the manufacturing strategy, and the product design itself. They'll all be driven by the business strategy we're hammering out here, which in turn is driven by the voice of the customer."*

CHAPTER **4**

Integrating
the Strategy

Six weeks later Mike Perez, B&W's VP of Marketing and Sales, was deeply involved leading a meeting with his immediate staff. The topic: Project Innovation. "Our market research is showing a definite consumer preference—at the upper end of the market—toward less glitz and opulence and more functionality. They're asking for a multi-function writing instrument, but one that looks elegant and feels good to use.

"It's likely that B&W will undergo a major strategic shift as a result of this. The board of directors has given us preliminary approval to develop an entirely new line of products— and most likely new business processes—to meet this opportunity. We've got plenty of cash in the bank, and tons of talent. At this stage, we feel good about our ability to pull this off.

"Here's our working strategy for this initiative." Mike turned on the overhead projector, which showed:

Project Innovation—Strategy Statement

Mission

Design, manufacture and market a revolutionary line of multi-function writing instruments which will:

- Deliver the highest degree of customer delight in the industry;
- Sharply improve B&W's profitability and growth;
- Dramatically enhance B&W's image in the marketplace as an innovator and leader.

Method

Change whatever needs to be changed in order to accomplish this mission. No part of the organization is to be considered "off limits" to the dramatic changes that are anticipated.

- Product Development . . . will probably use processes that are radically new to B&W in the development of new products.
- Marketing & Sales . . . will probably price, advertise, and sell these products very differently from how they've ever done it before.
- Operations . . . will probably be tasked with achieving a level of precision and excellence in its manufacturing processes greater than has ever been attained within the industry.
- Finance . . . will probably be required to change not only the processes by which it measures the effectiveness of other departments, but also many of its own internal processes.

This strategy will evolve and may change frequently over time, and it will be updated as required. Further, each primary area of the business is tasked with developing its own strategic plan to meet the objectives of project innovation. In so doing, they are urged to use the process called quality function deployment (QFD), because it enables the voice of B&W's customers to be translated into B&W terms and to be linked—both vertically and horizontally—throughout the organization.

"*By now you've all had overview training on QFD,*" *Mike continued. "Well, the executive group isn't asking you to do something that they haven't done. As you know, we used QFD to define and prioritize this year's company strategy. With QFD, we've been able to translate what the customers are asking for—customer 'wants,' in the jargon of QFD—into terms that are meaningful to us—called the 'hows.' Another term is 'measures'—measures that the customers use to know we're listening to them—and in QFD these are the* hows *plus their associated target values. It's our job to figure out how we're going to achieve these* measures.

"*As our strategy statement says, we'd like to use the same QFD processes within Marketing to determine our strategies to meet what's being asked of us. Here are the measures that were developed." He turned on the projector once more.*

---

3 or more inks, 1 erasable
3 or more leads
No bigger than a large Montblanc
Eraser for lead and 1 Ink
Quick, easy instructions in less than 5 minutes
High-tech, expensive look and feel
Refills available within 24 hours

"*These measures came out of the first QFD matrix, the one for the overall Project Innovation strategy. We call this the Phase I House. As you know, these measures were directly driven by the voice of the customer—the results of our in-context market research. Now we'll use some of these measures in our planning; they'll enter our matrix as wants. Then we'll develop our own set of hows—the specifics as to how we'll meet these requirements. And one of the very strong aspects of QFD is that, as we do this, we'll still be linked back into the voice of the customer.*"

*I*t's not enough to capture the voice of the customer and tie it into the company's top-level strategy. What's needed is a means to tightly link the overall strategy into the specific functional strategies for marketing, manufacturing, product development, etc.

Imagine a head football coach who layed out the game plan for next Saturday's contest against the Wildcats, but failed to share that plan with his assistant coaches. In the meantime, the offensive backfield coach developed his own game plan in a vacuum, as did the offensive line coach, the defensive coordinator, and the guy who looks after the special teams. None of these plans tied together. The result? The Wildcats won, 50–3. (The 3 points came about after a Wildcat fumble on their own 12-yard line.)

Now we can all pat ourselves on the back, secure in the knowledge that we don't do it that way in business. *But let's not be too sure.* Time and time again we have seen strategic plans calling for Marketing & Sales to go in one direction, Operations in another direction, and Product Development in a third. The plans for the individual functions didn't tie together; they were not mutually reinforcing.

The QFD process provides the essential linking capability. It does this by using the *measures* (*hows* plus target values) from the Phase 1 QFD House (the overall strategy matrix) as *wants* for the functional strategy matrixes. As shown in Figure 4-1, the *measures* from the Phase I House—the Business Unit Strategy—are passed into the Phase II Matrixes as *wants*. And please note also that the lines from the Phase I House are coming from the *bottom* of the house; this means that not only the *hows* but also their target values cascade into the Phase II Matrixes.

Let's look at how the Marketing & Sales team might proceed with their task. In developing the marketing strategy to

FIGURE 4-1: Linking the Overall Business Strategy into the Functional Strategies

Phase I QFD House:
The Business Strategy

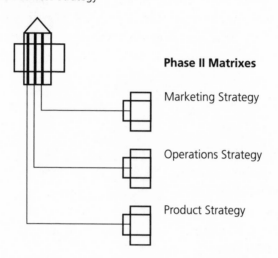

Phase II Matrixes

Marketing Strategy

Operations Strategy

Product Strategy

support the new product, they need to address topics such as distribution channels, advertising and promotional approaches, role of the sales force, and customer service/ order entry/order-fulfillment issues.

The team is focusing on the *measures* that were discovered in the Phase 1 House and have become *wants* that B&W needs to satisfy. Using the QFD process, they would typically go through the following steps:

1. Identify the relevant *measures* from the Phase I House, and treat them as *wants*.
2. Brainstorm *hows*, to meet the identified *wants*.
3. Set the relationships.
4. Calculate values and set priority rankings.
5. Do additional matrixes as required.
6. Develop the strategy, identify actions, and document.

Now we need to look at each one of these steps and get a bit more focus on what's involved.

1. *Identify the relevant* measures *from the Phase I House.* These *measures* become *wants* for the Phase II Matrix, which will address marketing strategies. For simplicity, let's assume that this meeting of the marketing/sales group is focusing on customer service issues, looking at two *wants*:

Refills available within 24 hours.

Quick, easy instructions understandable in less than five minutes.

Remember, these were identified in the Phase I House as potential breakthroughs because the competition was doing such a poor job.

Rarely, if ever, will all of the *wants* from Phase I be passed into any one of the Phase II Matrixes. There are several reasons for this:

- The company as a whole needs to focus on those *measures* that are new, immediate, or difficult—and carry those forward into the Phase II Matrixes. A *how* that is being done already, or isn't needed for two years, or is very easy to do will typically not "make the cut" for inclusion into a subsequent matrix.
- There will be multiple matrixes in Phase II: one or more for each of Product Development, Marketing, Operations, etc. Each of these areas will capture those *measures* which relate to what it does.

2. *Brainstorm* hows, *to meet the identified* wants. In our example, to meet the *want* of understandable instructions in less than five minutes, the marketing folks identified these *hows*:

Written instructions easy to understand
Instructions available over the phone at no cost

Next the team identified the following *hows* to meet the *want* of refill availability within 24 hours:

Mail order
Phone order
Retail store

In this step, which typically deals with only a few *wants*, it's a good idea to bring more *hows* into the process than back in Phase I. In other words, it's okay to be a bit less restrictive. In our example here, while it may be fairly obvious that mail orders will not satisfy the customer want of getting refills in 24 hours or less, the team may have elected to include it for completeness and to compare other *hows* against it.

3. *Set the relationships.* Relationships are the degree to which a *want* is impacted by a *how*: strong, medium, weak, or nonexistent. The matrix in Figure 4-2 shows the relationships that were set by the marketing team. Let's look at a few of these, and in so doing, we'll see a bit more about how QFD works.

RELATIONSHIP 2A

How: Written instructions
Want: Quick, easy instructions, understood in less than 5 minutes
Relationship: Medium. The team felt that written instructions for a device this complex, while necessary to include with the product, would probably not do the total job well enough

FIGURE 4-2: Relationships Between *Wants* and *Hows*

WANTS vs. MEASURES Legend

Strong	●	9
Moderate	O	3
Weak	△	1

		A - Quick, easy instructions understood in less than 5 min.	B - Ease of acquiring refills — received in 24 hours or less
1	Instructions for use		
2	Written instructions	O	
3	Instructions over the phone no cost	●	
4	Refills		
5	Available by mail order		△
6	Available by phone order		●
7	Available at retailer		△

RELATIONSHIP 3A

How: Instructions over the phone, at no cost

Want: Quick, easy instructions, understood in less than 5 minutes

Relationship: Strong. Verbal instructions, with the opportunity for questions and dialogue, were seen as more effective than written instructions. The customers should not have to pay for a phone call to get this service

RELATIONSHIP 6B

How: Refills available by phone order

Want: Ease of acquiring refills—received in less than 24 hours

Relationship: Strong. Phone ordering makes a next-day delivery possible. The customer would need to pay a premium for the fast delivery service, but the capability would be there. (The team initially felt the cost would be prohibitive, but after discussion they concluded that the time and costs involved in getting to a store that may be out of stock anyway might lead many people to willingly pay for the premium freight.) Standard delivery would be pegged at one week, with a lesser charge for shipping and handling

The team assigned a weak weighting to Relationship 7B, refills available in retail stores against 24-hour availability. This method is the standard industry practice and is theoretically the best. However, distribution can be spotty, and retailers frequently run out of stock. Thus an item that should be available on demand could have a lengthy order-fulfillment time. The team did recognize that retail distribution could probably work in concert with the telephone approach.

Is a given relationship strong, medium, weak, or nonexistent? Very often, people will have different views here: Tom says the relationship is strong, Dick says it's medium, and Harriet says it's weak. What to do? Well, what are the rest of the team members saying? If a majority of the team is saying "medium," that's the conclusion. The ideal outcome is unanimity, but a more practical goal is consensus. The team members need time to discuss, dialogue, be persuasive, and also to have their minds changed.

Further, one simple ground rule here can make the relationship setting task less burdensome: If the debate is over whether a relationship is weak or nonexistent, call it nonexistent and go on to the next one. This approach won't affect the final outcome materially, and it makes the process much more efficient.

4. *Calculate values and set priority rankings.* Figure 4-3 shows that two *hows*—the one dealing with instructions over the phone and the one on ordering refills over the phone—scored the highest. And there's a common thread running through them: the telephone.

5. *Do additional matrixes as required.* The telephone capability—both for instructions and for ordering refills—was becoming more and more important in the minds of the marketing team. It's quite likely that, in this situation, an experienced QFD facilitator would "apply the brakes" a bit, to keep the people from becoming too carried away with the magnificence of their discovery. One way to do this is to create another house, thereby enabling the people to sharpen the focus and gain more details on the topic, and to "bulletproof" their idea.

FIGURE 4-3: Weighted and Ranked *Hows*

WANTS vs. MEASURES Legend

Strong	●	9
Moderate	○	3
Weak	△	1

		A - Quick, easy instructions understood in less than 5 min.	B - Ease of acquiring refills — received in 24 hours or less	Weighted Value	Ranked Value
1	Instructions for use				
2	Written instructions easy to understand	○		3	3
3	Instructions over the phone no cost	●		3	1
4	Refills				
5	Available by mail order		△	1	4
6	Available by phone order		●	9	1
7	Available at retailer		△	1	4

Figure 4-4 depicts the two highest-ranked *hows* from the prior house being brought in as *wants* to this house:

1. Instructions for use provided over phone in less than 5 minutes, at no cost.
2. Refills available over the phone, delivered in less than 24 hours.

More brainstorming would be done about how to meet them, which could identify potential *hows* such as provide a toll-free telephone number, take telephone calls collect, provide a toll-free fax number, and provide a phone line with modem for computer-to-computer ordering. The weighted values in Figure 4-4 show that the 800 number voice hotline was clearly the best *how*.

Let's look at Relationships 5A and 5B. They're both strong. The telephone approach will require resources: trained people and telephone lines. Why couldn't these same resources be used as the main order entry point for refills? Further, depending on how the product is to be marketed, this same sales resource could be used for the OmniPen, the product itself. This is an example of a discovery—a breakthrough—that can come about as a result of the effective use of QFD.

Let's recap. The 800 hotline *how* was identified in the brainstorming session as a way to support the customer *want* of getting understandable information in less than 5 minutes at no charge (derived directly from the original customer *want* of being easy to use). Multi-functionality may lead to complexity, which of course is counter to ease of use. The 800 hotline would be a way to satisfy the customer *want* of easy to use; when the customer has a question, he can call the hotline.

However, and here's the important point, the 800 hot-

FIGURE 4-4: Additional Matrix — To Gain More Focus

WANTS vs. MEASURES Legend

Strong	● 9
Moderate	○ 3
Weak	△ 1

	1 Take collect calls	2 B&W voice	3 Fax machine	4 Provide 800 #	5 B&W voice	6 Fax machine
A - Instructions for use provided over phone less than 5 min., at no cost		○	△		●	△
B - Refills available over the phone, delivered in less than 24 hours		○	●		●	●
Total Value of Action		6	10		18	10
Ranking of Action		4	2		1	2

line also has a positive relationship with another customer *want*, that of being able to order refills and get them within 24 hours. What we're seeing here is that one *how* can affect a number of *wants*, not only the one for which it was originally identified. With QFD, it's much easier to see reinforcing relationships like this.

One last point: don't be reluctant to generate additional matrixes if it's felt they may be helpful. Often these are needed in order to gain more "granularity," i.e., a more focused and more specific insight into the issue at hand.

6. *Develop the strategy, identify actions, and document.* The process of setting strategies is fundamentally one of judgment, experience, industry knowledge, and it often requires quite a bit of courage—a willingness to look risk in the eye without blinking. QFD, or any other technique, will not develop the strategic plan but it does enable effective priority setting, a high degree of teamwork, and intense customer focus in strategic decision making. Most important, it greatly increases the odds of uncovering breakthrough discoveries.

In our example here, the 800 hotline would need to be evaluated externally for specific customer reactions and internally for practicality, cost, and resource requirements. If it clears these early hurdles, it could become a centerpiece of the marketing strategy for the OmniPen.

ELEMENTS REVISITED

This is perhaps a good point to revisit our four elements of innovation identified in Chapter 1 and relate them to what the B&W people are experiencing:

Element #1: Customer Issues—Service, Delight, Meeting and Exceeding Their Expectations—Need to Be the Prime Mover of the Business. Notice how the "voice of the customer" has remained in focus and at the center of B&W's thinking as they've developed their plans.

Element #2: The Executive Team Produces Products. These products—the strategies, plans, directions—are critically important. They have great leverage and high impact throughout the total organization.

Element #3: Executive Productivity and the Quality of the Management Product Are Critical Competitive Variables.—It's highly likely that B&W executives and managers, using these tools, are making more decisions per unit of time. It's almost certain that they're of far higher quality than before.

Element #4: The Executive Team Needs Superior Processes to Produce Superior Product. The tools we're seeing in this book—advanced market research processes, the use of QFD to set strategies, and another still to come, Strategy Deployment—are the executive equivalent of operational level techniques such as Statistical Process Control, Pareto Charting, Just-in-Time, and others. These tools enable senior managers to see through the complexity that is part of business in the 1990s, to gain insight into what their customers really want, and to sort out effectively how to meet those wants.

> **MYTH: American executives aren't capable; They're inferior.**
>
> **FACT: American executives can be, and often are, as**

good as or better than any others in the world. But they need better tools to do their jobs in the competitive pressure cooker of the 1990s.

THE TOOLS IN ACTION:
Functional Strategy Development via QFD at
Hewlett-Packard's Instrument Systems Division

Based in Fort Collins, Colorado, Hewlett-Packard's Instrument Systems Division has been producing voltmeters for quite a long time. Over the years, the business has rolled along without much happening in terms of innovation—or growth. In fact, some market share had been lost to a strong competitor.

However, a major recent initiative—using QFD extensively—resulted in significant changes in how HP Fort Collins approached the voltmeter marketplace. Two elements of their new marketing strategy are particularly instructive.

Faced with a price decrease by a key competitor, HP studied its Choice Modeling data base (see Chapter 2). The conclusions:

1. Doing nothing would result in lost sales.
2. Lowering the price to match the competition would retain volume but reduce revenue.
3. Holding the current price while *increasing the warranty* from one year to three years would actually gain market share—even in the face of the competitor price decrease. Thus volume and profits would increase. (With a mean time–between–failure of about thirty years, the additional cost for an additional two years of warranty would not be great.)

Using QFD, the people in the voltmeter business unit were able to "peel back several more layers of the onion." They learned that a major irritant to customers was, in those rare cases when a voltmeter failed, having to wait to get the unit repaired. This resulted in another major change to the warranty policy: when a voltmeter under warranty fails, the customer calls HP, who ships them a brand-new unit to arrive in less than 24 hours. The customer returns the failed unit, and the customer's credit card number protects HP in the interim. Customers are *delighted*.

A second major change in the marketing strategy concerned distribution channels. Voltmeters had historically been available only from HP and, as such, were less convenient to buy than the competitors' products. The QFD process helped the team to see the need for a radical change here, which resulted in an entirely new distribution approach. HP voltmeters are now available from retailers such as Micro-Age.

Results: For the voltmeter business unit, customer delight, a significant gain in market share, and higher profitability. For Hewlett-Packard as a corporation, the ability to leverage off the Fort Collins experience and transfer this knowledge into different parts of the corporation. Other HP divisions, including the premier Laser Jet printer business unit, have revamped their marketing strategies to include the features developed at Fort Collins.

SUCCESS FACTORS: DOs and DON'Ts

DO provide support and encouragement to all the teams involved in this strategy-setting process.

DO insist that the voice of the customer remain at the center of all discussions for all teams. Jerre Stead, the CEO at NCR, has a good way to achieve this: "In any NCR meeting, if the customer hasn't been mentioned for fifteen minutes, we stop and refocus the discussion."

DON'T forget about the second and third success factors from the last chapter—training and facilitation. They also apply here.

Let's look in on a subsequent meeting of B&W's Project Innovation team. Charlie the CEO is reading the proposed marketing strategy and talking at the same time:

"Well, isn't this interesting? What this is telling us is that we could have this 800 hotline—an industry first, by the way—to support our customers using our product, and also sell refills. Hey, wait a minute! Maybe we could sell the product itself via the same channel. Mike, how would the retail trade react to us selling direct?"

"Charlie, I'm not sure but I don't think it would be a problem," Mike said. "There's not a strong element of exclusive territories or channels in our business, and catalogue distribution is common. Basically the trade's happy if they can get the product when they want it, keep their inventories low, and see the product fly off their shelves without having to firesale it. But definitely, if we decide to go ahead with this, I'll check it out with some of our key accounts."

Fran asked, "Mike, why not let the trade order our products via the same 800 hotline? This would help them reduce their inventories, avoid stockouts, and thus make our total product line more attractive to them?"

"Super! I think they'll be real happy with that kind of trade-off."

"Why are you guys talking about selling product via an 800 number?" asked Owen. "My understanding is that this number would be available to people who've already purchased the product."

Harry spoke up. "Referrals, for one. I can just see someone sitting on a plane, using the product, and recommending it to the guy next to him. Having the number right there— maybe imprinted on an interior part of the pen—could get us some business. Shoot, they've got phones on planes now—the guy could call the 800 number right away and have the pen the next day."

"Harry, that's right," said Mike. "Further, our strategic marketing plan for OmniPen calls for heavy print advertising, in publications targeted for upscale business and professional readers. This includes the airline magazines. Their readers are exactly the type of people who are the customers for this product. These ads could contain the 800 number and pitch the twenty-four-hour service."

"I'd like to hear from some others of you," Charlie interjected. "Paul, where do you people in Product Development stand on all this?"

"Well, as you know, Charlie, we've created a multifunctional product design team for the OmniPen. It includes some people from my department, naturally, but also folks from Marketing, Manufacturing, Purchasing, Finance, and several suppliers. They're utilizing the same kind of Concurrent Engineering approach we've used before.

"What's new is that they're using QFD for this project, and it's very different. They're coming down the learning curve, struggling a bit, having fun, and feeling very good about being able to avoid the situation we had last year when we did

a great job designing a new product that the customers didn't want to buy. One of them said that for this product, we've got a lock on the voice of the customer and we're not going to let go. In fact, we've just about decided that we'll need to do more market research in several very specific areas; we need more focus on some of the specifics.

"And the teamwork is even better than before. QFD— because its focus is centered on the customer—really helps to pull people together. It helps to get rid of the politics and the tunnel vision. I can remember when I played football at Grambling, I thought we had the best teamwork imaginable. Well, our OmniPen product development team is as good as we were back then. It's impressive."

"That's great, Paul. Thanks. Owen, how about Operations? Has QFD helped your people?"

"It sure has," said Owen. "My reaction is the same is Paul's: it really helped us cut through the politics and internal wrangling. I mean, how can somebody argue effectively against things that the customer wants, merely to protect his or her own turf? Not very well.

"Our QFD Matrixes show a priority to produce at very tight tolerances—higher than anything we've ever done before. This understanding is central to everything that we've put together. Okay, here's our strategic plan to support Omni-Pen, and as you can see, it has two major elements: factory focus and supplier partnering.

"First, we plan to dedicate all of Plant 2 to OmniPen production; we feel it's necessary to create what's called a focused factory because of the requirements for precision and tight tolerances. To make it work, we need people and equipment dedicated solely to this task, giving it 110 percent of their concentration and effort. This is going to result in enormous changes for the people involved: new job assignments, new

reporting relationships, different ways of doing things, some jobs going away, and so on.

"Second, for the time being we'll be outsourcing a high percentage of OmniPen components. We've concluded we need to forge much closer ties to suppliers for OmniPen than we've ever done before. This has already started, thanks to Paul and the product design team, involving what will likely be the two primary suppliers. This partnering process will accelerate as we enter production, and will represent an entirely different approach to how we do business with our suppliers.

"Would we have arrived at these same two strategic directions without using QFD? Maybe, maybe not. But even if we had, I can guarantee you that it would have been a whole lot more difficult, would have taken longer with much more kicking and screaming, and the details of these strategies would have been watered down with compromises. One of the team said it very well: 'QFD helps people to accept common sense.'"

"Is there any bad news, Owen?" asked Fran.

"Yeah. Resources. We're running much leaner than just a few years ago, and we already have a lot on our plate. We continue to spend a lot of time on Total Quality; we're deeply involved in the Quick Changeover project; we've got supplier certification; with your folks, Fran, we're implementing activity-based costing; the ISO 9000 project is under way; and Harry's people in HR have us looking at a major revision to the compensation plan. Those are just the big projects; there are dozens of smaller ones under way. And, oh yeah, I almost forgot one other thing."

"What's that?"

"Shipments. Every month we have to produce and ship X million dollars worth of product."

Charlie smiled. "Thank you for remembering, Owen. So

what you're saying is that shipments are job 1, plus we've got all these other things to do. Now we're going to layer on top of that all of the OmniPen stuff. I don't think we as a company can do it all at one time. This stuff has got to get prioritized. I was talking to one of the faculty guys over at Chapel Hill the other week and he had a great quote: 'When everything's important, nothing's important.'

"This leads me to question how we've done strategic planning in prior years. We've generated new plans, which required us to assign tasks with little thought given to what was not going to get done. Some good people, faced with an overwhelming agenda, either give up or burn out. Inadvertently we've given our people tasks exceeding reasonable limits. And I'm convinced that's one of the reasons why we haven't done a good job recently in executing our strategic plans.

"Charlie, you're 100 percent right," Owen responded. "We have to avoid that pitfall. But we're already part of the way to the solution: QFD has really helped us do effective high-level prioritization. What we have to do now is integrate the strategic plan for OmniPen into our overall business strategy, and let the priorities line up as they will. And we can do that.

"However, I don't think that's enough. We shouldn't mandate all this from on high; we can't just push it down if we want it to work. I believe we need a tool to get lots of our people—not just a few—involved in determining what to work on and how much time to devote to one initiative versus another. Trouble is, I don't know if such a thing exists."

"Owen, it may," Mike said. "Do you remember my daughter Paula, the industrial engineer at Boeing? Well, she was telling me about a process Boeing uses to deploy strategies. She says it's very focused and also very participative at the same time. It's very similar to what they taught us at that seminar I went to last winter."

CHAPTER 5

Deploying the Strategy

*For the next few months, things were quite busy at the B&W
office and plants. Widespread training was conducted, involving many more people than the QFD training recently
completed. Terms such as "PDCA," "catchball," and "cross-
functional" were heard frequently.*

*In general, the training went quite well. B&W's prior
efforts in TQM and other initiatives paid dividends here as
most of the employees had acquired a good base of knowledge
and a degree of comfort with the training process itself.*

*Numerous meetings were held, sometimes involving only
two people: an employee and his or her boss. Some of these
meetings were difficult; some were heated; most were positive
and cooperative, ending in smiles and handshakes. Harry
Simon and his people in Human Resources kept a close watch
on the proceedings and provided significant help to those working through difficult issues. Let's see what the B&W folks were
up to.*

Most companies have problems when trying to execute
strategies; they find it difficult to *deploy* them throughout the
organization so that they can actually be accomplished. See if
any of the following sound familiar:

- *It's hard to get buy-in from all of the many different people and departments who need to be involved.* Lack of commitment means lack of results, thus the strategy is not executed properly.
- *People frequently get overloaded.* There are simply too many things to be done in the time available. When everything's a top priority, nothing's a top priority, therefore the strategy is not executed properly.
- *Different functional areas of the business have different priorities.* Thus those initiatives which require cross-functional cooperation and teamwork often come up short. When different departments are at cross-purposes, the strategy is not executed properly.

It's a wonder that any strategic plans ever get executed well. In actual fact, most of them don't. The success rate of strategy execution—of implementing new business initiatives very well—is about on a par with launching new products: terrible. What we have here is an *execution gap*, a failure to deploy and execute strategic plans.

MYTH: American workers are lazy and inferior.

FACT: American workers can be, and often are, as good as or better than any in the world. But they are only as good as their leadership.

Larry Huston, manager of Total Quality for Procter & Gamble's Worldwide R&D Program, says it well: ". . . most executives do not understand their responsibility for honing and managing *a process* for strategy implementation." He goes on to point out the need for executives "to translate their notions of what needs to be done into specific manageable strategies and targets that can be *robustly deployed* throughout the organization."[1] (Emphasis ours)

The Wall Street Journal reports:

Strategies fail because managers don't understand.

That's the view of top executives who formulate the objectives that somehow get lost down the corporate ladder. A survey by consultant Booz, Allen & Hamilton finds that only 37% of the senior officials think other key managers completely understand new business goals. Only 4% of the top bosses think middle managers totally understand.

Not surprisingly, compliance drops with understanding, to the point where nearly half the top executives believe that middle managers go along with new strategies at best partially or not at all.[2]

MYTH: All that's needed is to empower the people in the offices and on the plant floor. Give them good tools and processes, and the results will take care of themselves.

FACT: True empowerment comes only when people understand and buy into the strategic direction of the business.

TURNING STRATEGY INTO ACTION

Here also, as with the use of QFD for strategy development, the tools do exist for deploying and executing strategy effectively. They're being used successfully today by a wide range of organizations in North America, including Boeing, Dow Chemical, Hewlett-Packard, Procter & Gamble, Texas Instruments, Xerox, smaller companies like Baldrige award winner Zytec. Ellen Domb, a consultant based in Upland, California, says: "We've seen these processes used successfully in large organizations and small, public sector as well as private, organizations delivering either services or products or both."

We call this *Strategy Deployment*. Strategy Deployment is the delivery system for the Management Product. It enables companies effectively to:

- deploy strategic plans throughout the organization;
- obtain buy-in from people at all levels in all departments;
- avoid overloading people with more tasks than they can reasonably be expected to accomplish;
- facilitate cross-functional teamwork and cooperation; and
- measure progress, then take corrective action when actual performance is behind plan.

Strategy Deployment enables companies to keep the entire organization *aligned* on achieving strategic breakthroughs. This alignment is critically important. In most manufacturing companies, for example, it's essential to have a logistics system which will drive matched sets of components into the finishing operations, so that the product can be built and shipped. It's equally important and perhaps even more challenging for all companies, not just manufacturing, to drive *linked and balanced sets of activities* throughout all departments, so that the strategy can be executed effectively.

Few companies are able to do this well. If one were to survey 1,000 organizations, the results would probably show that several hundred of them do little strategic planning worthy of the name. Many more do some form of strategic planning. However, within this group, a large majority have an unstructured, unfocused approach to execution; a hundred or so use Management By Objectives

(MBO); and one or two (each, not hundreds) use Strategy Deployment (see Figure 5-1). The competitive potential of Strategy Deployment is very high, on two counts: one, it works better than any other approach; and two, few companies in North America are using it.

FIGURE 5-1: Approaches to Strategic Planning and Execution

1. Strategic planning done	• Strategy Deployment *(Hoshin Kanri)*	BEST
2. Strategic planning done	• Management By Objectives (MBO)	↑
3. Strategic planning done	• Execution Unstructured or Nonexistent	↓
4. Strategic planning not done	• No Execution	WORST

Strategy Deployment vs. MBO

Let's take a look at Management By Objectives (MBO), which has been used with good results by many organizations throughout the world. It is, in fact, the basis upon which the Japanese developed Strategy Deployment (*Hoshin Kanri*). Why, then, do we view it as inferior? After all, both MBO and Strategy Deployment start at the top of the organization; both break objectives down into smaller increments while attempting to maintain alignment among them; both consider results to be very important; and both review progress periodically. So there are quite a few similarities between the two approaches, but in fact the differences are far more significant.

The table on page 108 points up these differences.

In summary, MBO and Strategy Deployment have some similarities; both attempt to achieve the same goals. However, Strategy Deployment, an outgrowth of MBO, is far

MANAGEMENT BY OBJECTIVES (MBO)	STRATEGY DEPLOYMENT
Focuses on results	Focuses on both results and the means to achieve them
Is a top-down process; most often objectives are delegated	Starts at the top, but provides a bottom-up component—feedback, negotiation—necessary to get commitment at lower levels in the organization
The subordinate is responsible for developing the means to meet the objective	The manager and the subordinate work *together* to determine what's necessary to achieve the objective
Focuses on individual or departmental performance in the achievement of objectives	Recognizes that most of the work on strategic breakthroughs is done cross-functionally, by teams, and thus goal congruence must be maintained among all parts of the organization
Measures progress by tracking results	Measures progress by tracking performance against the plan. However, Strategy Deployment also concentrates on diagnosing what went wrong, understanding the cause-and-effect relationships involved, fixing the processes that need fixing, and learning from the experience so that the problem will not recur
The objective is a contract for a given level of performance	The objective is the expected outcome of the plan—fully understood and committed to

superior. An analogy from the world of military aviation may be helpful here. The F-9 Cougar was a good aircraft for its time, the 1950s: a transonic, carrier-based fighter with machine guns, rockets, bombs. Today, it wouldn't stand a chance against its great-grandson, the F-14 Tomcat, which possesses Mach 2+ performance coupled with 1990s electronics and weapons systems. These planes look somewhat similar; they each have wings, engines, three wheels, and a tail hook. But there's a world of difference in effectiveness.

No one would want to go to war today in a forty-year-old aircraft. MBO is management equivalent of the F-9 Cougar, and Strategy Deployment of the F-14 Tomcat. Which one do *you* want to take into the industrial warfare of the 1990s and beyond?

THE THREE C'S OF STRATEGY DEPLOYMENT

The essence of Strategy Deployment revolves around the "three C's": CA-PDCA, Catchball, and Cross-Functional Linking. In effect, they're the three legs that form the foundation for Strategy Deployment. Let's look at each one in turn.

CA-PDCA

Thanks to the Total Quality explosion that's occurred over the last twenty years, many people are familiar with the PDCA cycle (see Figure 5-2). These letters stand for PLAN, DO, CHECK, ACT; the process they represent is an important foundation upon which Total Quality is built. It's often referred to as the "Shewhart Cycle" or the "Deming Cycle," after its developers.

The PLAN phase sets the objectives and lays out the activities necessary to achieve them. DO is implementing

FIGURE 5-2: The PDCA Cycle

the plan. Nothing new so far—people have been doing this for centuries.

The next step—CHECK—is where the PDCA approach really helps, and it reflects the fact that implementations don't always go exactly according to plan. Frequently, when this happens, organizations engage in one or more of the following:

1. They play "Who Shot John?" In other words, "Let's find the culprit, the guy who caused this to get messed up . . . and then we'll nail him!"
2. They give up.
3. They start all over.

They may go through this process a number of times. They PLAN, they DO, they PLAN, they DO. They never get beyond DO, and that's all right if all of the implementations are successful on the first pass. But most often they're not.

Playing "Who Shot John?", giving up, going back to the drawing board—these are not a part of PDCA. Rather, CHECK the results of DO. Evaluate these results to determine whether the objective has been reached. If it has, press on or go to another issue. If not, analyze the situation to determine what caused the shortfall. The ACT step calls for determining the appropriate action to correct the situation, and to reenter the PLAN phase with the necessary modifications.

Many Total Quality practitioners state that there is no best place to enter the PDCA cycle. Their approach says to start anywhere, because the cycle is self-correcting and will bring you to where you want to be. This is often the case.

But not with strategic planning and execution. It must start at the CHECK stage. A company's strategy has enormous impact on the entire organization: its well-being, its health, its very survival. There is simply too much at stake to start anywhere other than with careful analysis of the company's current situation, the competitive climate, and—most important—what the customers want.

This fact—the critical need to "do one's homework" up front—has led to an extension of the classic PDCA cycle into CA-PDCA. The first two letters refer to CHECK and ANALYZE. These are essential steps prior to entering the PLAN phase. From then on, the standard PDCA process takes over until the next annual planning cycle begins. At that point, the CA part of CA-PDCA kicks in one more time.

Let's now ask how the CA-PDCA cycle relates to the B&W example we've been following throughout this book. How will B&W make use of this CA-PDCA approach? Well, they already have. They've already gone through the steps of CHECK, ANALYZE, and much of PLAN as it relates to their Project Innovation/OmniPen initiative. They used first-rate market research and QFD to do this, as we saw in Chapters 2, 3, and 4.

What remains is for B&W to deploy their strategic plans for OmniPen throughout the organization, so that these plans will be executed effectively. To do this they will use Strategy Deployment techniques, which are based on classic PDCA. And since B&W has been active in Total Quality Management, of which PDCA is a key element, this will not be a totally foreign process to them (see Figure 5-3).

Catchball

Catchball means two-way communications: feedback and dialogue. It's negotiation—back and forth, like tossing a ball—but with structure, based on facts. Catchball makes two major contributions to the Strategy Deployment process:

1. It facilitates buy-in widely throughout the organization. This is because the goals are not dictated from on high, but rather are *negotiated* between supervisor and subordinate.
2. It highlights issues of resource and priority. It helps to neutralize the problem of overload, where people are required to take on more projects than they can possibly

FIGURE 5-3: The CA-PDCA Methodology

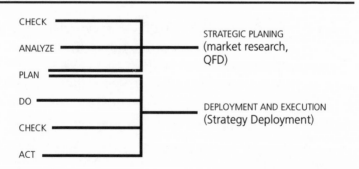

Note that PLAN is a component of both STRATEGIC PLANNING and DEPLOYMENT AND EXECUTION. Planning occurs at both the strategic level and at the tactical level of deployment and execution.

handle. Here also, it's the informed negotiation aspect of Catchball that makes the difference.

Most companies have a problem with this workload issue, and today it's worse than it's ever been. The approach they've followed, as the business climate has become more competitive, is to load more and more projects onto their people. To make matters worse, the number of people has not increased or even remained constant. It's decreased as companies have downsized and delayered and the workload has gone up. Resources have gone down and the results, as Charlie Evans pointed out, include failure to execute the strategic plan and people burning out.

With Catchball, it's essential that the boss not mandate objectives and tasks. Phrases like "Well, just do what you need to do," "I'm sure you can handle this," or, "If you can't get this done, I'm sure we can find somebody who can," should be considered off limits. Reality can be a pain but it must be allowed to rear its ugly head in this process. If reality is taken into consideration—via informed, fact-based discussion—then the strategic plans have a good chance of becoming more than a collection of wish-lists. They can become achievable action plans against which people can legitimately be held accountable.

There is, of course, another side to this. The Catchball process cannot be allowed to water down the strategic objectives merely to turn them into easily achievable action plans. Then the overall strategic plan won't be met. It's the boss's job to work with her team, to help them prioritize, to reallocate resources where necessary, and thereby develop action plans that are attainable and fit the overall strategy. Note: unlike QFD, Strategy Deployment is normally a manual process, not involving a computer. See Appendix B for examples of forms used Strategy Deployment.

Do strategies ever get modified as a result of Catchball? Yes they do, but typically the amount of change isn't great. And sometimes, modification is found to be essential. Let's look at B&W again for an example of this.

1. *Carol Collins, B&W's customer service manager, has participated in the development of the strategic plan for the Marketing Department.*

2. *She discusses the OmniPen strategic plan with Otis Smithson, Order Department Supervisor. (A graphic representation of this and the ensuing communications is shown below in Figure 5-4.) Otis will play a significant role in the establishment of the 800 hotline; he will be the "owner" of this portion of the overall OmniPen initiative.*

    Otis expresses concern at the amount of change that will be required of his department. Despite Carol's reassurances that additional people will be provided to man the 800 hotline, Otis feels the issue goes deeper than merely adding people. He's worried about his capabilities, and those of his section heads, to provide the time, mental focus, and leadership to implement such a major step properly

FIGURE 5-4: The Catchball Process

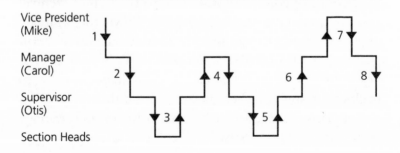

Vice President (Mike)
Manager (Carol)
Supervisor (Otis)
Section Heads

and effectively. *In other words, he's not sure they can do it right; he's worried about embarrassing himself, his people, and his company.*

Carol asks Otis to develop one or several scenarios under which he would be comfortable in taking on the challenge of the 800 hotline.

3. *Otis meets with his section heads and others in his department. They discuss, dialogue, brainstorm. They come up with two plans, A and B, which are presented to Carol.*

4. *Carol has concerns about Plan A, which she feels would result in delaying the start-up of the 800 hotline. However, she likes Plan B a great deal; it gets the job done—and it's* their idea. *But there's a catch: Plan B calls for deferring a major project within the Order Department, which is necessary to support the new sales analysis reporting system. This is tough, because Carol knows that the new system has been a pet project of her boss, Mike Perez. Carol asks Otis for a Plan C.*

5. *Otis meets with his people, and after some more brainstorming, concludes that they can keep the sales analysis project moving forward, at about one third the current rate of progress, if they can get 60 hours per week of temporary help to free up some of their people's time.*

6. *Carol says it looks good to her but she'll need to clear it through her boss because of the delay in the sales analysis project.*

7. *Carol talks to Mike, who says all right. Mike recognizes the overriding importance of the OmniPen project, and is willing to wait a bit longer for the sales analysis system to come up.*

8. *Carol passes the good news on to Otis.*

*C*atchball means top-down/bottom-up, and negotiation. Therefore Catchball is iterative. Managers communicate the strategic plan to their people, the people communicate back to their managers. This communication upward could be good news: "Great, boss, no problem. We'll handle it." Or, as with Otis and Carol, it identifies a problem: "We're going to have trouble doing this, boss, because of . . ." And, of course, the process continues until action plans are agreed upon.

Cross-Functional Linkage

Most major strategic initiatives and breakthroughs involve more than one function. Therefore it's essential that Catchball move horizontally as well as vertically. Thus, as with QFD, cross-functional teams are utilized in the Strategy Deployment process.

In the example of B&W's Customer Service Department, it's likely that they would have some people on their team from outside the department, specifically Purchasing, Production Control, and perhaps Distribution. These people, most likely managers, would be there to enable horizontal Catchball to work.

Why would horizontal Catchball be needed? Well, if the customer *wants* to be able to get refills within 24 hours Carol and Otis and their people in the Order Department are tasked with achieving that objective, but they can't get the job done all by themselves. They could develop the greatest 800 hotline capability anywhere, but still not fill the customers' orders on time due to lack of product—or an inability to get product packed and shipped quickly.

Cross-functional teams address this all-too-common problem head on. In our example, the Purchasing representative on the Customer Service team would be charged with providing 100 percent availability on purchased refills. He or she would need to take that requirement back to the OmniPen deployment team centered in Purchasing (which possibly has a Customer Service person on it). Ditto for Production Control (for in-house manufactured refills and also possibly for OmniPens themselves) and for Distribution (to ensure that Shipping will be able to pick, pack, and ship in a very short time).

It's likely that some form of horizontal Catchball would take place in these cross-functional processes. Other functions may need to be brought in at some point, perhaps Systems or Finance. These discussions would be structured negotiations, using the linking and display capabilities of the QFD Matrixes and the Strategy Deployment forms to maintain focus and not lose sight of the overall goals of meeting and exceeding the specific customer wants.

An excellent way of displaying an entire plan is shown in Figure 5-5. Someone working on a given action plan can see how his task plus others at that level will result in the accomplishment of the next-higher action plan. For example, let's say that action plan 1.3.1 (to the right of the page) refers to the establishment of the 800 hotline. This would be supported by the items below that. Action plan 1.3.1.1 might refer to what the Order Department needs to do for the 800 hotline implementation; items 1.3.1.2, .3 and .4 could refer to the respective action plans for Purchasing (sourcing, negotiating, and contracting with the refill suppliers), Production Control (scheduling refills from suppliers so that they're always available), and Distribution (shipping refill orders to customers very quickly).

Frequent progress reviews assure that progress is being made at the right pace or, alternatively, highlights a problem that needs to be rectified. *Please note*: the nature of

FIGURE 5-5: Displaying the Total Strategic Plan

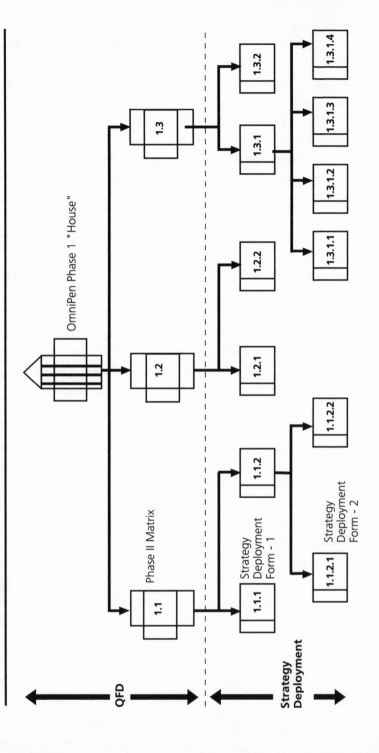

these reviews is that several people share information about an activity of importance to both of them, identify impediments to their mutual goal, and revise the plan as necessary. This process has been referred to as "supportive, linked and shared."

Using the cross-functional approach, an effective display of information, and supportive progress reviews enables integrated plans to be deployed to the detailed level. Developing and executing *linked and balanced sets of activities* throughout the organization—to support the strategy—is one of the things that separates the winners from the losers.

To sum up, Strategy Deployment—the delivery system for the Management Product—represents quite a different process from what many people have become accustomed to over the years. The communication and the buy-in that Strategy Deployment can bring to a company will be hard to get without, first, initial training in the process and then continuing reinforcement by senior management. This means that the "same old way" of forcing projects down throughout the organization—with inadequate communication and without buy-in—cannot continue.

DAY-TO-DAY OPERATIONS

Strategy Deployment processes are not intended to be used for everything. Rather, they work best when used to support a few major strategic breakthroughs. Ongoing activities—shipping product, reducing emissions, making continuous improvements in quality and productivity—are best handled via processes to support day-to-day operations. These aspects are sometimes called "daily management," and this is where much of the PCDA process is employed.

But here also, in the ongoing operation of the business, there's good news. Another important tool for the executive team, this one called Sales & Operations Planning, is being used with excellent results by many companies. This process forms a crucial linkage between the strategic, top-level plans of the organization and the day-to-day, week-to-week, month-to-month running of the business. Sales & Operations Planning is described in Appendix C.

Let's take a moment to view the overall flow of the Strategy Deployment process, as depicted in Figure 5-6. The customer-integrated strategic plans, created with the help of QFD, are passed to Strategy Deployment.[3] Catchball and Cross-Functional Linking take over at this point to negotiate how the breakthrough priorities will be accomplished. This workload must be balanced with that coming from day-to-day operations, so that both the strategic breakthroughs and the day-to-day running of the business can be accomplished successfully.

THE TOOLS IN ACTION:
Strategy Deployment at Blue Cross/Blue Shield of Northeastern Pennsylvania

The United States is currently in the throes of a major reengineering of its health care delivery system. It's widely felt that the current system is "broken" and that major changes are necessary.

There are, however, bright spots in the health care landscape, and one of these is Blue Cross/Blue Shield of Northeastern Pennsylvania (BC/BS NEPA), headquartered in Wilkes-Barre.[4] It has a reputation as one of the most progressive and cost-conscious of all of the seventy-three Blue

FIGURE 5-6: Designing and Delivering the Management Product

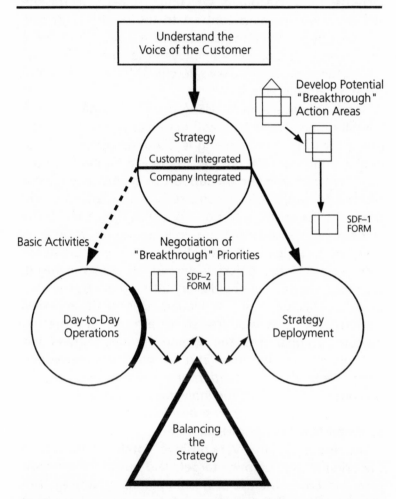

Cross Plans in the United States. BC/BS NEPA employs over 600 people and serves over 600,000 people in an area characterized by high unemployment, virtually no population growth, and customers who are extremely cost-conscious.

BC/BS NEPA does a fine job of strategic planning, referring to its major strategic initiatives as "Blue Chips." For

1992, Blue Chip #1 was to achieve moderate premium rate increases for its customers, well under 10 percent. This objective stands in sharp contrast to the double-digit rate increases by most health insurers in recent years. To achieve this objective, BC/BS NEPA employed the kinds of Strategy Deployment processes we've described here, referring to them as "Hoshin Planning."

Here's Tom Ward, BC/BS NEPA president and CEO: "The overall supportive, linked, and shared environment that is called for in Hoshin Planning is the underpinning of the deployment planning portion. There is a tie between deployment planning and the supportive environment that is created through other means, such as Leadership Workshops . . ." He goes on to point out that their CFO "is the leader of the Blue Chip 1 Hoshin Planning effort. In turn, each task has a leader. Catchball was done to assure alignment to tasks and objectives across all teams involved. Supportive reviews are held every three weeks by the Blue Chip 1 leader with all task leaders. During those review sessions, each task is addressed in terms of its projected outcome compared to the original targets. Barriers and difficulties are identified and action plans developed where needed. *The intention and spirit of these review sessions are to support the individual and to improve and modify as needed the process by which the tasks are being accomplished.*" (Emphasis ours)

The results to date? Very positive. Totally on track with the original Blue Chip #1 targets laid out in the strategic plan. Moreover, the use of Hoshin planning (Strategy Deployment) led the Blue Chip #1 team to an important discovery: the product line would need to be changed significantly to make further progress. Thus the Blue Chip #1 initiative has carried over into 1993 and 1994 in order to drive the necessary changes.

SUCCESS FACTORS:
Dos and Don'ts

DON'T inhibit the Catchball process. The negotiation and the give-and-take must be allowed to occur. This process is radically different from what's gone before; trust will take time to build but it can be shattered in an instant. Therefore . . .

DON'T make decrees from on high. Rather, make suggestions and identify opportunities for compromises. Be flexible.

DO get training on Strategy Deployment for yourselves and all other people in the organization who'll be involved. Further, training in team processes is necessary; if this hasn't already been provided, it should be combined with the training on Strategy Deployment.

DON'T have too many Strategy Deployment projects going on at one time. Keep the number down to one or two to start. Remember, day-to-day operations takes care of most of running the business; QFD coupled with Strategy Deployment generates the breakthroughs.

It's time to check on how B&W fared using the Strategy Deployment Process for OmniPen.

Some months later, B&W's executive team was getting together in preparation for the annual stockholders' meeting. Charles Evans said, "So we're agreed then that we'll make the OmniPen product launch the centerpiece of the annual meeting. Owen, will you have product to give each one of the attendees?"

Owen (Operations): "Yes sir. We're gonna give 'em the top

of the line model: the 18k gold-plated one. These were production prototypes but they've all been carefully inspected. They're 100 percent, Charlie."

"And we're ready to do the formal product introduction three weeks later," added Marketing VP Mike Perez. "That's the print advertising, direct mail, press releases, the whole bit. We'll start shipping to the trade about one week ahead—right, Owen?"

"You bet."

Silence for a bit. The team reflected on how far they'd come in such a short time, using the new tools. The scope of their accomplishment—and the speed at which it was done—felt really good. Harry pointed out that six months ago—he wouldn't have thought it was possible, and his comment got wide agreement. Then Charlie spoke up. "For the annual meeting, what would you folks think about having employees themselves tell the OmniPen development story? These would be people from all levels and all parts of the company, and they could tell about their role in launching OmniPen."

"Charlie, that's a super idea." said Harry Simon. "And I'm not just saying that because you're the boss. It's great. We could ask some of the people to tell about some of the discoveries, the breakthrough ideas, the 'ahas' they experienced as the lights turned on."

"Such as?"

"I can talk to that," Mike said. "There was a real struggle in the Order Department. Carol and Otis and their people were enormously impacted by OmniPen: the 800 hotline, dealing with retail customers for the first time, a massive time compression in processing orders and getting product shipped—from days to hours. Well, you all know how we kid Otis Smithson about being from England and therefore resis-

*tant to change? Otis became one of the biggest change agents
in the company; he's been wonderful.*

"*Otis will tell you—and I'm sure he'll be glad to tell the
stockholders—that this never could have happened without
the Catchball and the cross-functional capabilities that we
gained through Strategy Deployment.*"

"*Otis is one possibility, and how about somebody from your
area, Owen?*" *asked Paul Lewis.*

"*Well, we can certainly get some production folks from
Plant 2. They're really pumped up over there. Incidentally,
they're after me now to change the name of the plant to
OmniPen Central. They claim they don't like being called
number two.*

"*Another possibility is Purchasing. As a matter of fact, the
Purchasing story may be a good one. Pete Jaworski and his
people have done a complete reversal, from feeling over-
whelmed to being totally in control of their destiny. For years
I've had a running gun battle with Pete over workload and
priorities. Pete always complained that they had too many
projects to do any of them well. He was always bugging me for
priorities. When OmniPen came along, it almost sent him
round the bend—it was so big and there was so much Purchasing involvement.*

"*Well, I think Pete was a lot more right than I was.
Actually, Charlie said it here in this room some months back:
we've overloaded some of our people and haven't given them
good priorities. Pete can tell the stockholders how Strategy
Deployment helped us to deal with the capacity issue—the
overload problem—and also to prioritize which project was
most important, which the second most, etc. It was very reas-
suring to Pete and his people that what we were asking them to
do was totally aligned with our overall business strategy. And
that—thanks to QFD—was completely in sync with what*

the customers were telling us. Pete's a believer now, and I can tell you that Purchasing is a major factor behind the progress that Operations has made on OmniPen."

"If we're passing out bouquets, Human Resources should be cited for the super job they did," said Fran. "They really helped a lot of our folks over the rough spots in learning the Strategy Deployment process."

Harry nodded a thank you.

"This is a stockholders meeting, so we don't have a lot of time," Paul said. "How about if we have two or three live presentations of, say, five minutes each and then project a series of slides with quotes from other people? Wrap up this part of the meeting in about twenty minutes. Charlie, it's your show—what do you think?"

"Let's do it. We've got a real story to tell."

CHAPTER **6**

Taking Ownership
of the Tools

Delta Flight 348, inbound to Atlanta from San Francisco, was about two hours from touchdown. Mike Perez and Owen Barnes were comfortably settled in their seats, heading home from a successful West Coast sales trip to promote OmniPen. It had been a very productive week; the airline lunch was actually edible; life was good.

Owen turned to Mike. "Michael, as you know, I grew up with this company. I began hanging around the plant with my dad when I was six years old, and started sweeping the floor when I was eight. B&W's in my blood. And I just want to let you know how grateful I am for your getting us started on Project Innovation and OmniPen. I absolutely believe we saved the company, and you got us started. Thanks a million."

"Well, thank you, Owen. I really do appreciate that." As with many American males, Mike had a tough time accepting compliments. He quickly deflected to conversation. "But, you know, in looking back I can see we were fortunate, because we more or less had a roadmap of what to do. Without that I don't think we could have made it. We made the right choices at pivotal times."

*M*ike's right. B&W *was* fortunate, and we need to talk about how to reduce the luck factor for your company. In other words, how should a company go about this total process of understanding the voice of the customer, linking that voice into the company's strategy, and deploying that strategy successfully? An important question, indeed.

IMPLEMENTATION

Broadly, there are two ways to implement these processes, which we'll label Plan A and Plan B. Plan A is the total approach. It includes robust market research, setting the overall strategy and the derivative functional strategies via QFD, and using the Strategy Deployment process covered in Chapter 5 for execution. This is the route that B&W followed, although—as Mike Perez indicated—they didn't have a completely clear vision of the entire process before they began.

Plan B represents a scaled-down approach. Compared to Plan A, its market research component, while solid, is less robust. The usage of QFD is about the same; but the strategies are executed via the company's current processes, not via the Strategy Deployment method we've described here. Let's first look at Plan A in some detail.

Step 1: Executive Briefing. A high-level overview presentation to top management and other key people who will be involved, lasting about half a day. The purpose here is to equip these people with enough knowledge of the processes that they can make informed decisions about them.[1]

Step 2: Initial Training. Initial training—two to three days—on capturing the voice of the customer, Quality Function Deployment, using QFD to set strategy, and

Strategy Deployment. This will provide the executive team and others with the necessary knowledge base.

Step 3: Customer Day. To focus on which market research methods will be used, develop an action plan, make assignments, and launch the market research phase. One day, same team.

Step 4: Conduct Market Research. To capture the voice of the customer. It may include focus groups; it should include in-context visits; it may include work with choice models. As we said earlier, it's particularly important that the executive team members themselves are directly involved with the in-context customer visits. The B&W folks did a good job here but, as we'll see, they may decide to do even more in the future.

Step 5: Develop Strategies Using QFD. Concentrating heavily on new, innovative, breakthrough initiatives. This normally occurs in a several-day session. Done by the team.

Step 6: Conduct Training on Strategy Deployment. For the executive team and all members of Strategy Deployment teams. The formal training itself is typically a series of one-day sessions. Some companies will begin this step prior to developing the strategies (Step 5), so that after the strategies are developed, they can be deployed quickly. Training on teaming processes and the basic quality tools may also be necessary here if it hasn't already been done.

Step 7: Execute the Strategies. Use the Strategy Deployment techniques of Catchball, Cross-Functional Linking, etc. Track progress. Adjust the action plans as required. Make it happen. Execute.

The total elapsed time, from start to finish, typically ranges from four to eight months. Major areas of cost are training and facilitation, typically in the mid-five-figure range, and the market research, which can range from a low of about $15K, to cover the cost of travel for in-context visits, up to a quarter million for computerized text analysis and Choice Modeling. For the small to medium-sized organization, most early projects of this kind will involve market research costs in the mid-five-figure area. For example, the Hewlett-Packard voltmeter project cited earlier, which was enormously successful, spent $37,500 for market research.

For Plan B—the scaled-down approach—the elapsed time and training/facilitation costs tend to run about half to two thirds those of the total approach. Market research costs typically are confined to the costs of travel for the in-context visits.

The positives from the scaled-down approach are that it takes less time and money, while still yielding excellent results in producing the Management Product. In our experience, this approach is attractive to smaller organizations. It also provides a somewhat less elaborate introduction to the process, enabling a company to evaluate its effectiveness prior to making a larger commitment of time and money.

ELEMENTS OF INNOVATION—ONE MORE TIME

At the start of this book, we defined four elements of innovation. Let's review these briefly once again.

Element #1: Customer Issues—Service, Delight, Meeting and Exceeding Their Expectations—Need to be the Prime Mover of the Business. Peter Drucker's words from many years ago bear repeating: "What people in any business think they know about customers and markets is more likely to be wrong than right." And further, "It is the customer who determines what a business is. What the customer thinks he is buying, what he considers 'value,' is decisive—it determines what a business is, what it produces and whether it will prosper."

If Drucker is correct—and most informed people believe he is—then is it any wonder that we've been having problems industrially? Many of our businesses have an incorrect understanding of their customers. This must change, because *it is the customers who determine what the businesses become and whether they'll prosper.*

Element #2: The Executive Team Produces Products. The Management Product—strategy, direction, leadership—is the output of a process. The process of producing it is subject to many of the same factors that apply to other production processes. The executive team produces these products for their internal customers—the rest of the people throughout the company.

These people—the American workers—are as good as or better than any in the world. But they are only as good as their leadership.

Element #3: Executive Productivity and the Quality of the Management Product Are Critical Competitive Variables. The need for transformational change is as great or greater in the executive suite than on the plant floor or in the offices. Much progress has been made in terms of quality and productivity here, to the extent that high product quality is often no longer a differentiator.

All of these things being equal (and they're rapidly becoming so), the race will be won by the company whose executive team delivers its Management Product more effectively and with higher quality.

Element #4: The Executive Team Needs Superior Processes to Produce a Superior Product. The Total Quality revolution has, for the most part, neglected top management. But their need for better tools is acute. And the good news is that these tools—the ones we've presented in this book—already exist. They're proven; they're not expensive by today's standards; they're easy to understand; and, although they require some hard work, they're not difficult to use.

SUCCESS FACTORS:
DOs and DON'Ts

Here are some DOs and DON'Ts that apply to the total process.

DON'T try to delegate. The Management Product can be successfully developed and delivered only by the top management of the company.

DO "lock" onto the voice of the customer. Keep your customers in focus. Talk about them at least once every 15 minutes.

DON'T be rigid and inflexible, particularly in the Strategy Deployment process. The Management Product tells people where we're going. Once people understand that, they want to have a say in how we're going to get there.

DO be prepared to work hard, to have fun, and to gain insights into your business that you've not seen before. Be prepared to start concentrating on problems of growth rather than contraction.

SUMMARY

What we've presented here is a focused look into the future of management. The tools, the processes, the methodologies we've covered will become more and more widely used. Using these processes will become a standard part of how top management does its job—along with the business plan, the budget, and MBWA. More and more organizations of all types will use these techniques. The business schools will teach them. And we believe this will happen *before the year 2000.*

At that point—when the critical mass of organizations are using these processes—they'll still be necessary, in order to stay even or to catch up. But, let's face it, they will no longer provide a competitive advantage.

However, between now and then, companies that use these leading-edge tools effectively will have an enormous advantage over their competitors that don't use them. The benefits—delighted customers, higher market share, increased profit, stable employment, and happy investors—are being achieved today by many of the organizations we've cited.

Here's Leo Burke, Director of Training for Motorola's Land Mobile Products Sector: "Motorola's been well known for its successes in achieving very high (6 sigma) quality levels. Well, that's great—but it's not enough. Within Motorola, we're in the process of transforming ourselves from a technology-driven company to a customer-driven company. And QFD, front-ended by first-rate market research, is making that transformation possible. I don't believe we could do it without these tools."

One last time, let's see how the B&W people are doing. *About nine months later, the B&W executive team was meeting to discuss plans for the OmniPen victory party. The mood in the room was jubilant, and the prevailing sentiment was to make this the biggest celebration in the company's history.*

Things had indeed gone well. The OmniPen launch had been executed without a major hitch, and only a few minor ones. Marketplace acceptance of the new product had been very good. "Almost too good," commented Owen Barnes at one point as his Operations group struggled to meet customer demand in excess of even the optimistic, high-side sales forecast.

Production rates were ramped up slowly, as B&W steadfastly refused to compromise product quality. This was communicated to customers, who were told that their order would be shipped one or several weeks in the future due to the unexpectedly high demand.

Customer service was not allowed to suffer either. There was a brief period when OmniPens were not being shipped due to a shortage of the specialized eraser involved. This shortage was caused by priority being given to supplying refill orders, a topic of heated debate within the company. Some Production people, and some in Marketing and in Finance, had a real problem with shutting down the OmniPen production line merely to ship refills.

The issue went to Charles Evans, who "broke the tie" in favor of the refills, saying, "We promised our customers we'd deliver refills in twenty-four hours or less. We never said we'd ship new product that quickly. Sure, we'd be better off in the short term shipping fifty-dollar products rather than fifty-cent erasers. But we're in this ball game for the long run. Our goal here is to build an enduring relationship with our customers."

A positive financial impact from OmniPen had not yet been felt, reflecting the fact that cumulative volume was short of the break-even point. But break-even would soon be reached, and profit projections for the upcoming quarters showed a substantial boost from OmniPen. The stock price was up 15 percent from a year ago, reflecting these projections and OmniPen's impact in the marketplace. Fran Collier and Brenda Kelly had been designated a two-person task force to look for potential acquisitions, and had identified some attractive candidates.

"Well," said Charlie, "after we throw this big party, what are we going to do for an encore? What's next?"

"I hope we don't just sit around and wait for a good acquisition to come along," said Fran. "Things are encouraging at this early stage, but these are usually long-drawn-out deals."

"Well, we do need to make a decision on the OmniPen line extension downward into the student market," Paul chipped in. "We believe there's significant volume potential there, but as Mike pointed out the other day, there's the risk of eroding the OmniPen image with a lower price product."

Mike: "You bet. Plus it seems to me that this student market is a whole different animal. You could see some of that in the market research we did for OmniPen. But it's a big market, no doubt about that. I think if we go into it, we shouldn't view it as a line extension to OmniPen. It should have a separate identity, maybe a separate team within the company."

"So what are we waiting for?" This from Charlie.

"Charlie, we can't make a decision on this. There are too many unknowns."

"So what are we waiting for?" Charlie repeated.

"Huh?"

Harry smiled. "I know what he's getting at, Mike. What he's saying is why don't we use the same processes we used for OmniPen to really get a handle on this student crowd. We've got the tools; let's use 'em!"

"Yeah!" said Mike. "Why not? We have better top management tools—the advanced market research, the QFD, the Strategy Deployment—than anyone in our industry east of the Pacific Ocean. Let's capitalize on this strength."

"We should start right at the beginning," Paul said, "with a series of in-context visits just like last time. Only now we focus strictly on the student market. Then I'd like to see us do some Choice Modeling. We didn't do that for OmniPen, and we certainly could have used more insight into how our customers actually make their buying decisions.

"You know, I heard a term recently: 'future quality.' It's the opposite of 'historical quality,' which means to develop the product, ship it, send out questionnaires to find out how badly we screwed up, and then reactively try to fix what's wrong. Future quality means to find out from the customers ahead of time what delights them and what makes them unhappy. Then proactively develop the total product to deliver the former and avoid the latter. I think we did a pretty good job on future quality with OmniPen, but I'm convinced we can do better if we have better customer data.

"Anyway, after we see what we've got from the market research, we can use QFD to help us make our decisions and set our strategy."

"Paul, that's great," Owen responded. "Right on the mark. Further, we should make these tools a standard part of how we do our jobs, just like the business plan and the budget. The OmniPen success cannot be a 'one-night stand.' For *example, we haven't yet addressed most of the wholesaler and retailer 'wants' that we got last year—things that apply to all of our product lines like on-time deliveries, no split shipments, no invoicing errors, etc. These wants should flow right into our strategic planning process."*

Fran spoke up, "Absolutely. The question we should routinely ask ourselves is not: should we use these tools. Rather, we should ask: Are we currently using these tools and, if not, why not? We need to move this strategic planning process from being a point event that we do once a year to a continuous process. We've got to imbed these things in our brains, or we'll forget about them."

"Use 'em or lose 'em."

"Right. We should have a motto: 'Nothing starts until we get the voice of the customer.' "

"Charlie, how does all this sound to you?"

Charlie smiled. "So what are we waiting for? Let's do it."

And they did.

Were they successful this time around? We don't know. That's perhaps another story.

Were they certain of success as they got started? We don't know that either, but we hope not. Arrogance is a particularly destructive virus, most often attacking the successful.

What we do know is this: B&W's odds for success with the new initiative into the student market are high, thanks to the leading-edge tools and processes they're using. They used them for OmniPen, and were successful—in much the same way that the real-world companies we've cited have been successful.

The B&W executive team is well along the learning curve.

They'll consistently outperform their competitors who don't use these tools—just as an F-14 pilot will consistently outmaneuver and outshoot a guy flying a forty-year-old F-9.

We wish B&W were a real company, and publicly traded. We'd like to be stockholders.

APPENDIX A

Software Sources

1. QFD/Capture—QFD Data Management Program for DOS, Windows, and Macintosh computers.

   International TechneGroup Incorporated
   5303 DuPont Circle
   Milford, OH 45150
   (513) 576-3993

   Note: This is the software used to generate all of the matrixes used as examples in this book.

2. QFD designer—QFD software for Windows-based computers.

   Qualisoft Corporation
   7395 Bridgeway West
   West Bloomfield, MI 48302
   (313) 626-4070

Examples of Strategy Deployment and Forms Used

Note: The description of Strategy Deployment described in this appendix covers the baseline processes only and does not detail a solution for all situations. This process is customized for each company. How each step is accomplished is not described either. The reference is to the general flow; the way action occurs at each step is beyond the scope of this appendix.

STRATEGY DEPLOYMENT OVERVIEW

Strategy Deployment is important to ensure that work to support company strategy decisions is acted upon.

Its goals are to assure that:

1. Results occur for the strategies discovered;
2. Actions are linked across the company in accomplishing those results.

Strategy Deployment enables actions to meet strategies that accomplish key customer measures of *wants* and *needs*. It is important to understand that the term "customer" comprises the full spectrum of customers, both internal— the "voice of the *company*"—and external—the "voice of the *customer*."

Strategy Deployment adds value to the Strategy/QFD process by:

1. Providing a structured and systematic support effort for multi-functional teams in accomplishing goals and objectives;
2. Providing a method to check the effectiveness of the action plans developed.

In our B&W example, the need is to communicate and assure success for the addition of an 800 number to be used both for acquiring information on how to use the writing instrument and to order refills.

B&W management would use the Strategy Deployment processes and the form used in that methodology to link and track that effort. The fact that the strategy planning process raised this 800 number as a high-priority issue indicates the need for a structured approach. All other data of less priority would be accomplished and tracked using day-to-day approaches.

THE STRATEGY DEPLOYMENT PROCESS

Translation from Strategy Planning to Strategy Deployment

B&W management would make a final company *and* customer balanced decision on the planned accomplishment of key strategy issues uncovered in the **strategy planning** process. It would then transfer these from the planning matrixes to the SDF-1 form (see Figure A-1). This form documents the following data:

FIGURE A-1: Strategy Breakthrough Planning Form (SDF – 1)

Date   For Year

Key Customer Measure (*How*) by Rank	Target Value as of this date	Management Assigned Owner

Associated Customer "*Wants*"	Relationships	

Competitive Data

Us

Key Customer Measures (*"Hows"*)—by priority from the last QFD Matrix. Included in this data would be the *Target Values*—those understood as of the last matrix developed. These could change based on new research but really should represent targets that will support customer "delight."

Management Assigned Owner for defining and planning and accomplishing the results required.

Associated Customer "Wants" link the team processing customer requirements that are seen as driving these strategies. This provides information on potential links to other departments and efforts involved in successfully accomplishing these goals.

By noting the strength of the *Relationships* that management saw between the measure (*"How"*) and the *"Wants"* and *"Needs,"* the SDF-1 form documents the thinking of management in making its choices of strategy.

Competitive Data from the QFD chart alert the team to competitive positioning already understood by the management team in making the strategy decision.

Translation from Breakthrough Plan to Actions

The SDF-2 **Breakthrough Objectives** form (Figure A-2) serves to identify objectives by focus. In our example, the team delivering the 800 number would identify the *objective* of defining and planning the most realistic actions, in light of company day-to-day and breakthrough objectives to provide this capability. (A separate process for balancing these resource issues is utilized but not described here.)

The team is chartered realistically to define all actions

FIGURE A-2: Strategy Breakthrough Planning Form (SDF – 2)

Date _____ For Year _____

Key Priority Customer Measure (*How*) Identified

Target Value as of this date

Supporting Action to Accomplish	Owner of the Objective	Date Required

required and to evaluate the potential for accomplishing them. This is done through detailed planning activities outside the scope of this form, which would result in development of the *Supporting Action* documented on SDF-3 (Figure A-3) as **Performance Tracking Data.** This form is used to ensure the accomplishment of action agreed upon between the team responsible and the management team.

The SDF-4 **Deviation Report** (Figure A-4) would be used formally to identify and recommend actions required to ensure success in accomplishing the strategic breakthroughs planned.

Figure A-5 graphically describes the steps outlined in this appendix.

FIGURE A-3: Strategy Breakthrough Performance Tracking Form (SDF – 3)

Date

Key Priority Customer Measure (*How*) Identified

Target Value as of this date

Supporting Action to Accomplish	Performance Measure	Target Limits	Review Period	Owner

Copyright © 1993 by Bill Barnard

Appendix B

FIGURE A-4: Strategy Breakthrough Deviation Report Form (SDF – 4)

Date
Key Priority Customer Measure (*How*) Identified Target Value as of this date
Supporting Action to Accomplish
Issue
Situation that existed when deviation occurred   Date
Cause — method used to determine
Short-term solution in force
Plan to assure that the problem will not recur
Results of the solution
Other issues as a result of this problem

FIGURE A-5: Strategy Deployment

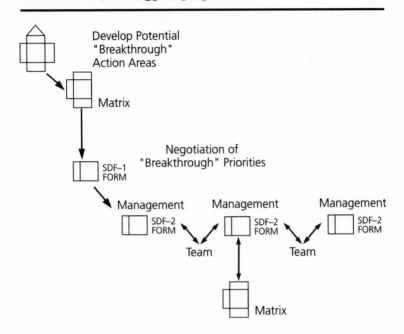

APPENDIX C

Sales & Operations Planning

Sales and Operations Planning (S&OP) enables top management to proactively manage customer service levels, inventory investment, and lead times for fulfilling customer orders. As such, it represents their "handle"—their direct control—over these strategically important aspects of operating the business.

In many companies, on-time delivery performance, inventory levels, and customer-order lead times are not well planned and managed. As a result, customer service is poor, or the inventories are too high, or the order backlog is too long and customers are turning to the competition.

Because it enables companies to prevent these kinds of problems, Sales & Operations Planning is considered by many to be an indispensable tool for top management. Direct benefits include:

- improved customer service levels;
- shorter customer-order lead times;
- more stable production rates;
- lower inventories

A significant indirect benefit is that S&OP enhances teamwork among the executive group. The president of Abbott Labs U.S. Pharmaceutical Division commented that S&OP helped his vice presidents to "see the business through my glasses," in other words, to view the business holistically rather than in terms of their own individual functions of marketing, manufacturing, finance, etc.[1]

The S&OP Process

The most important element in this process is the top management S&OP meeting, which happens once a month. In this forum, each major product family is reviewed. The information (displayed in aggregate, not in detail) shows sales performance to forecast, production performance to plan, and the resultant inventory levels and/or customer order backlogs. (See Figure A-6 for an example of how the information is displayed.)

In this example, for a make-to-stock product family called Medium Widgets, the demand/supply strategy specifies a target customer service level (shipments on time and complete) of 99%. The target finished inventory necessary to support this shipping performance has been set at 30 days' (or one month's) supply. (See area **A**.)

Let's examine the 30-days' supply inventory target. Why does this company feel it needs 30 days of finished goods inventory? Answer: Its experience over the recent past has shown that 30 days is a minimum level necessary to provide 99% customer service. Should this 30-day supply target be considered as a constant, fixed far out into the future? Answer: Definitely not. The principle of Continuous Improvement should drive this company to improve its sales, production, and logistics processes so that 99% customer service is attainable with only, say, 25 days supply. And then 20 days supply. And then 15. But for now, the realities of life are that it takes a month's worth of inventory to provide the 99% service level.

In area **B**, actual sales are compared to forecast. For the past three months, sales are running ahead of forecast by

FIGURE A-6: Sales & Operations Plan for June 1994

FAMILY: MEDIUM WIDGETS (MAKE TO STOCK)
TARGET CUSTOMER SVC LEVEL: 99%

UNIT OF MEASURE: 000 UNITS
TARGET INV LEVEL: 10 DAYS ON HAND

SALES	MAR	APR	MAY	JUN	JUL	AUG	SEP	OCT	NOV	3RD 3MOS	4TH 3MOS	NEXT 12MOS	TOTALS FISC YEAR	TOTALS BUS PLAN
Forecast	100	100	100	105	105	110	110	110	110	345	345	1335	$12,770	$12,700
Actual	110	98	114											
Diff +/-:														
month	+10	−2	+14											
cum		+8	+22											
PRODUCTION														
Plan	100	100	100	105	110	115	115	115	115	345	350	1365	1272	1300
Actual	100	102	99											
Diff +/-:														
month	0	+2	−1											
cum		+2	+1											
INVENTORY														
Plan	50	50	50	30	35	45	50	55	45	45	50			
Actual	40	44	30											
Days-on-hand	8	9	6	6	7	9	10	11	9	9	10			
Cust Service %	97%	98%	89%											

Demand Issues and Assumptions
1. Forecast assumes no competitor price changes
2. Accelerated export demand will continue through middle of next year

Supply Issues:
1. June and July production plan represents maximum effort due to vacations

22M units on a cumulative basis. Actual production performance to the plan is evaluated in area **C**. It's close to being
perfect.

Area **D** shows inventory performance to plan, and the
actual customer service performance. We can see a serious
problem developing here: as the forecast was oversold, the
actual inventory dropped below plan. The result: customer
service has dropped to 89% for May, far below its 99% target.

The new sales forecast is shown in area **E**. Totals for the
next 12 months, and totals in dollars for the fiscal year,
ending in December in this example, appear here. The fiscal
year total is made up of both sales history (Jan–May) and
sales forecast (June–Dec). To the right are shown the fore-
casted dollars in the Business Plan. This latter allows for an
easy comparison between the Business Plan and the S&OP
forecast (often called the latest estimate, or LE) for the fiscal
year's volume. Based on this, the top management team
may elect to change the Business Plan accordingly. The
assumptions which underlie the forecast are listed in area **H**.

The future production plan, based on the new forecast
and other considerations, is shown in area **F**, and the relevant supply (production/procurement) issues are listed in
area **J**.

Area **G** contains the future inventory projection for finished goods. It shows that the target inventory of 10 days
on hand will not be reached until September.

In summary, Figure A-6 is an example of a proven, effective format for Sales & Operations Planning. The intent is
to have all of the relevant information for a given product
family on one piece of paper. There the S&OP display
shows a striking similarity to the QFD House; they look
very different, but they both show all of the important data
in one display.

Each product family's situation—both its recent past and its future outlook—can be viewed completely and organically. For decision-making purposes, this has proven far superior to displays of information which show only sales, or inventory levels, or production.

That's important, because the essence of the S&OP process is decision making. For each product family reviewed, a decision is based on recent history, recommendations from middle management, and the executive team's knowledge of business conditions. The decision may be:

1. Change the sales plan;
2. Change the production plan;
3. Change the inventory/backlog plan; or
4. None of the above—the current plans are okay.

These decisions represent plans agreed upon by the president and all involved vice presidents. They are documented and disseminated throughout the organization. They form the overall "marching orders" for Marketing, Sales, Manufacturing, Materials, Finance, and Product Development. (New product plans are reviewed within S&OP in terms of their impact on the demand/supply picture.)

These groups break down the aggregate plans from S&OP into the necessary level of detail: individual products, customers, regions, plants, and materials.

The total S&OP process, however, is not a point event that occurs in one two-hour, top management meeting each month. Rather, preliminary work begins shortly after month's end and continues for some days. This phase, called Pre-SOP, involves middle management and others throughout the company. It includes:

- capturing sales history, production data, and inventory/ backlog levels from the month just ended;
- updating the sales forecast;
- reviewing the impact of these changes on the production plan, and determining whether adequate capacity exists to support them;
- identifying alternatives where problems exist;
- formulating agreed-upon recommendations for top management regarding overall changes to the plans, and identifying areas of disagreement where consensus is not possible; and
- communicating this information to top management with sufficient time for them to review it prior to the S&OP meeting.

The information contained in Figure A-6, therefore, would represent the recommendation coming from the Pre-SOP team to top management regarding Medium Widgets. It is then top management's job to make a decision: accept the plan as submitted, or change it. In the example in Figure A-6, the below-target inventory levels in June through August may be viewed by top management as unacceptable, because the company will not be providing good customer service. They may decide to incur the additional (perhaps substantial) costs of extreme overtime, or subcontracting, or bringing in temporary help, so that the inventories can get back on target sooner than September.

Thanks to Pre-SOP, the top management S&OP meeting should not take long; two hours or less is the norm with companies that do this well. The net result of S&OP for the top management group should be fewer meetings, less time in meetings, more productivity in their decision-making processes, decisions of higher quality, and an improved quality of work life. And most of the middle management people involved in the Pre-SOP process will experience the same results.

BENEFITS

Sales & Operations Planning helps to solve a number of nagging problems that many companies have struggled with for years. Here are a few examples.

Problem: "There's a disconnect between our top-level plans and what happens day to day. We in top management really have little control over what goes on at the detailed operational level on the plant floor, in Sales, and in Purchasing."

Solution: An important part of Sales & Operations Planning is to communicate the new plans, which have been tested in Pre-SOP for "doability," to the operating-level people. They are then held accountable for hitting these plans. And performance against those plans is measured and reported, each month.

Problem: "We're not consistent. We lurch back and forth between emphasizing customer service, which causes the inventories to go way up, and inventory reduction, which causes customer service to deteriorate. The executive who shouts the loudest determines the marching orders."

Solution: Sales and Operations Planning establishes, up front, the desired levels of customer service, and the inventories and backlog times necessary to meet them. Then top management, working as a team led by the president, manages these variables to achieve the company's goals.

Problem: "We need better control over our budget. We set next year's operating budget late in the fiscal year. At that point we have over twelve months of forward budget, which is our authority to spend. However, as the new year goes on, the amount of forward budget drops to nine months, then six, then three. But often we need to make spending commitments for things with longer lead times. Then we have to work around the system, and we can lose control."

Solution: Sales and Operations Planning is done monthly, goes out for 12 or more months, and can readily be translated into dollars. As such, it serves as a *rolling monthly update* to the Business Plan, hence the budget. These important elements in running a business can be kept far more current with S&OP. Further, S&OP can make creating next year's budget a lot easier.

Problem: "We're in a very seasonal business. Every year during the peak season we go through the same fire drill: late shipments, lost orders because of our long lead times, enormous amounts of overtime, and heavy training and lay-off costs. There's got to be a better way."

Solution: Sales & Operations Planning has helped companies in seasonal businesses to identify the relevant costs and benefits of more level production plans, make decisions on an informed basis, and then manage the business accordingly throughout the year.

Problem: "We've been meeting once per quarter to review the sales forecasts and make changes to the budget. However, that hasn't helped to solve our operating problems with demand and supply."

Solution: Sales & Operations Planning is a *monthly* process. Virtually all manufacturing business are too dynamic and fast-paced to recalibrate plans only once per quarter. Further, production plans and inventory/backlog plans need to be reviewed also, not just the sales plan.

SUMMARY

Many companies have difficulty in establishing a valid high-level game plan for sales, production, and inventory levels. Without valid plans, performance suffers: customer service is poor, or production is inefficient, or inventories are too high. Or all of the above.

Sales & Operations Planning is a tool that enables the top management team to establish in advance the desired levels of customer service, inventory investment, and lead times for customer-order fulfillment—and then to *manage the business proactively* to achieve that desired performance.

The results from the monthly S&OP process are driven downward to impact directly the day-to-day activities in sales, purchasing, and on the plant floor.

The results from the monthly S&OP process are driven upward, so that the company's overall Business Plan can reflect current realities and future plans. As such, S&OP is a pivotal process that *links* the top-level Business Plan with the day-to-day activities of running the business.

Sales & Operations Planning enhances teamwork among the top management group. Further, it has helped executives in charge of specific areas of the business—marketing, manufacturing, finance—to see the business more holistically, i.e., as a unit rather than a series of discrete functions.

Notes

CHAPTER 1: CRISIS IN THE EXECUTIVE SUITE

1. *International Quality Study*, 1992. Ernst & Young, Cleveland, OH.
2. *The Profits Versus Quality Survey*, 1993. The Quality Research Institute, Princeton, NJ.
3. *The PIMS Principles*, The Free Press, Robert D. Buzzell and Bradley T. Gale, (New York: 1987).
4. *Financial Times* (London), October 26, 1992.
5. *Money Magazine* (March 1993).
6. *Forbes*, April 26, 1993.
7. Now called AT&T Global Information Solutions. Since most readers will be more familiar with "NCR" we've elected to use that name throughout the book.
8. This is an advanced form of a more widely known market research technique, "Conjoint Analysis." Predictive Modeling/Choice Modeling can process a far higher number of variables than standard Conjoint Analysis.
9. Also known as Hoshin Planning, Policy Deployment, Management by Policy.

CHAPTER 2: UNDERSTANDING THE VOICE OF THE CUSTOMER

1. Peter Drucker, *Managing for Results* (New York: Harper Business, 1964).
2. Ibid.
3. Ibid.
4. Peter Drucker, *The Practice of Management* (New York: HarperCollins, 1954).

5. *Marketing News*, American Marketing Association, June 21, 1993.

6. The ten categories in the table are taken from an unpublished paper by Elemer Magaziner, a consultant based in Sedona, Arizona.

7. Drucker, *The Practice of Management*.

8. "The Wee Outfit That Decked IBM," *Fortune* magazine, November 19, 1990.

9. Reported on in detail in Edward F. McQuarrie's excellent book, *Customer Visits—Building a Better Market Focus*, New Park, CA: SAGE Publications, 1993.

10. *Fortune*, special edition (Autumn–Winter 1993).

11. Also referred to as "Choice Modeling."

12. Called "SUMM"—for Single Unit Market Model. This is a proprietary product developed by Eric Marder Associates, New York. The term "single unit" refers to the fact that each individual customer is treated independently, as a single unit.

13. The technique employed here was again SUMM: Single Unit Market Model.

14. See McQuarrie, *Customer Visits—Building a Better Market Focus*.

CHAPTER 5: DEPLOYING THE STRATEGY

1. Larry A. Huston, *Using Total Quality to Put Strategic Intent into Motion*. Planning Review Conference Summary, Planning Forum Conference, September–October 1992.

2. *The Wall Street Journal*, May 1, 1990.

3. The total *Hoshin Kanri* methodology contains a form of matrix analysis. Some companies use this instead of QFD for strategic planning, and this can work reasonably well. However, we believe it is less effective than our approach. One of the main elements of QFD's power is its intense focus on customers and their wants; this is what drives the generation of strategic breakthroughs.

4. For more information, see "Hoshin Planning in Blue Cross Northeastern Pennsylvania" reported in the proceedings of the

1992 GOAL/QPC Annual Conference. Available from GOAL/ QPC, 13 Branch Street, Methuen, MA 01844.

CHAPTER 6: TAKING OWNERSHIP OF THE TOOLS

1. This step might be skipped if all of the decision makers have read this book.

APPENDIX C: SALES & OPERATIONS PLANNING

1. David Rucinski, "Game Planning," *Journal of the American Production and Inventory Control Society* (First Quarter, 1982). This is an interview with the president of the U.S. pharmaceutical division of Abbott Laboratories, discussing their experiences with Sales & Operations Planning.

Glossary

BUSINESS STRATEGY The strategic plan for the total business unit. *See* functional strategies.

CA-PDCA Stands for: CHECK, ANALYZE-PLAN, DO, CHECK, ACT. This is the strategic version of PDCA. Processes for understanding the voice of the customer along with QFD are used in the Check, Analyze phase to set strategies. Strategy Deployment and day-to-day management processes are used in the PDCA phases. *See* PDCA.

CATCHBALL The phase of Strategy Deployment that involves dialogue, feedback, and negotiation. It enables the vertical linking of strategies and action plans up and down the organization, facilitates widespread buy-in, and helps to ensure that priorities are clear and that resources have been provided.

CHOICE MODEL Another term for predictive model.

CORRELATION MATRIX The "roof" of the QFD House. It shows positive and negative relationships between *hows*.

CROSS-FUNCTIONAL LINKING That aspect of Strategy Deployment that enables plans to be linked horizontally across the organization, i.e. throughout all functional areas of the business.

FUNCTIONAL STRATEGIES More detailed versions of the business strategy for the individual areas of the business: Marketing, Operations, Product Development, etc.

HOSHIN KANRI Japanese term for an advanced method of developing and deploying strategies. This process was developed in Japan.

Glossary

HOSHIN PLANNING Another term for Hoshin Kanri.

HOUSE OF QUALITY The primary QFD matrix. It is called this because its appearance often resembles a house with a peaked roof.

HOW The manner in which a customer *want* can be satisfied.

IN-CONTEXT CUSTOMER VISIT A method of gathering customer *wants* which observes the customers in their own environment and documents their expressed *wants*.

MANAGEMENT PRODUCT The strategies, plans, and leadership developed and delivered by senior management.

MEASURE A *how* with a corresponding target value.

PDCA PLAN, DO, CHECK, ACT. This process, sometimes referred to as the "Deming Circle," is one of the cornerstones of Total Quality.

POLICY DEPLOYMENT Another term for Hoshin Kanri.

PREDICTIVE MODEL An advanced form of market research that identifies customer choice patterns when the customers are choosing among real alternatives. The resultant data base is then used to simulate how customers would respond to changes in product, pricing, delivery, service, or combinations thereof.

QUALITY FUNCTION DEPLOYMENT (QFD) A rigorous method for translating customer *wants* into specifics that guide the company in its actions to meet those *wants*.

RELATIONSHIP The degree to which a *how* supports a customer *want*. Within QFD, these relationships can be strong, medium, weak, or non-existent.

STRATEGY DEPLOYMENT A process to transmit strategies and their attendant action plans throughout the organization, obtain buy-in, and track progress towards their achievement. It is based on the Hoshin Kanri approach, which originated in Japan.

TARGET VALUE The numerical representation of a *how*.

TEXT ANALYSIS Refers to computerized systems that process qualitative information—the voices of the customers speaking in their own words—to be reduced, combined, analyzed, and understood more easily and more objectively.

WANT What the customers desire in a product and/or service. Some *wants* are unspoken, because the customers aren't always aware of them.

Bibliography/Resource Section

Books on Strategy

Drucker, Peter. *The Practice of Management*. New York: Harper & Row, 1954.

_____. *Managing for Results*. New York: Harper Business, 1964.

Ohmae, Kenichi. *The Mind of the Strategist*. New York: Penguin Books, 1983.

Porter, Michael. *Competitive Advantage: Creating and Sustaining Superior Performance*. New York: The Free Press, 1985.

Ries, Al, and Trout, Jack. *Positioning: The Battle for Your Mind*. New York: Warner Books, 1986.

Wallace, Thomas F. *Customer Driven Strategy: Winning Through Operational Excellence*. Essex Junction, VT: Oliver Wight, 1992.

Books on Quality Function Deployment

Akao, Yoji. *Quality Function Deployment (QFD): Integrating Customer Requirements into Product Design*. Cambridge, MA: Productivity Press, 1991.

Barnard, Bill, and Daetz, Doug. *Building Competitive Advantage Using QFD: A Comprehensive Guide for Leaders*. Essex Junction, VT: Oliver Wight\Omneo Publishing, 1994.

Bossert, James. *Quality Function Deployment: A Practitioner's Approach*. Milwaukee, WI: ASQC Quality Press, 1991.

Books on the Modern Product Development Cycle

McQuarrie, Edward. *Customer Visits: Building a Better Market Focus*. New York: Sage Publications, 1993.

Reinertsen, Donald, and Smith, Preston. Developing Products in Half the Time. New York: Van Nostrand Reinhold, 1991.

Slade, Bernard. *Compressing the Product Development Cycle: From Research to Marketplace.* New York: Amacom, 1993.

General Interest: Modern organizational issues

Hampden-Turner, Charles, and Trompenaars, Alfons. *The Seven Cultures of Capitalism: Value Systems for Creating Wealth in the United States, Japan, Germany, France, Britain, Sweden, and the Netherlands.* New York: Doubleday Currency Book, 1993.

Hofstede, Geert. *Cultures and Organizations: Software of the Mind.* New York: McGraw-Hill, 1991.

Segne, Peter. *The Fifth Discipline: The Art and Practice of the Learning Organization.* New York: Doubleday Currency Book, 1990.

Significant Interest: Quality history and quality in America

Dobyns, Lloyd, and Crawford-Mason, Clare. *Quality or Else: The Revolution in World Business.* Boston: Houghton Mifflin, 1991.

Zuckerman, Marilyn, and Hatala, Lewis. *Incredibly American: Releasing the Heart of Quality.* Milwaukee, WI: ASQC Quality Press, 1992.

Index

Fidelity Magellan, 12
Focus groups
definition, 39
new ideas generated by, 39
shortcomings of, 18
Ford Foundation, Choice
Modeling at, 51–52
Functional strategy development,
see Quality Function
Deployment (QFD),
functional strategy
development via
Funder, as customer, 36

Gallagher, Susan, 46
Gibson, Larry, 47–48

Hearing and understanding the
voice of the customer, *see*
Customer, hearing and
understanding voice of
Hewlett-Packard (HP), 105
Choice Modeling at, 19
Customer/Strategy Linking
processes and, 20–21
functional strategy development
via Quality Function
Deployment at, 96–97
in-context customer visits by,
42–43
leading edge processes used by,
16
new product success at, 30
quality and productivity of
decision making at, 14
understanding customer at,
53
Hoshin Kanri, 107
Strategy Deployment and, 21
see also Strategy Deployment
Hows
brainstorming to meet identified
wants in, 85, 86–87
conflicts identified between, 61,
72–74

identifying, 61, 65, 66
target values assigned to, 61,
65–67
wants relationship with, 68–72,
73, 139
wants vs., 66
Huston, Larry, 104–5

IBM
NCR versus, 41
quality and productivity of
decision making at, 14
Idea generation, *see* Focus groups;
In-context customer visits
Idea testing, focus group for, 39
see also Choice Modeling
Implementation, 128–30
In-context customer visits, 19, 40–
46
at Black & Decker, 45–46
insights from, 52
to potential customers, 42
sales calls versus, 40–41
test analysis software for, 41, 43–
44
by top management, 42–43, 53
training for, 53
Innovation, *see* Elements of
innovation
Installer, as customer, 36
Integrating Strategy, *see* Quality
Function Deployment (QFD),
functional strategy development via
Intermediate user, as customer,
37

Kano Model, 34–35
Kano, Noriaki, 34–35

Leading edge, processes as, 15–16
Lockheed, quality and productivity
of decision making at, 14
Lynch, Peter, 12

voice of; Quality Function
Deployment; Strategy
Deployment
Procter & Gamble, 104, 105
Customer/Strategy Linking
processes and, 20–21
in-context visits by Hewlett-
Packard to, 42–43
leading edge processes used by, 16
private-label products versus, 34
Product attributes, Kano Model
on, 34–35
Productivity, of top management,
13–15, 16, 95, 131
Proven, processes as, 16
Purchase decision, 33–39
see also Choice Modeling; Focus
groups; In-context customer
visits

QFD, *see* Quality Function
Deployment
Quality Function Deployment
(QFD), 57–80
at B & W Inc., 56–60, 77–83
breakthrough opportunity from,
61, 75
competition evaluated by, 61,
63–65
competition meeting measures
in, 61, 72, 74
customer identification and, 35
Customer/Strategy Linking
processes and, 20–21, 23
evaluation of, 74–75
expert facilitation for, 77
hows identified in, 61, 65, 66
measures in, 61, 65–66
at Pierce & Stevens, 75–77
in Plan A, 129
ranked *wants* in, 60, 61–63
relationship between *hows* and
wants in, 68–72, 73, 139
success factors in, 77
target values assigned to *hows* in,
61, 65–67

trade-offs among measures
identified in, 61, 72–74
training for, 77
Quality Function Deployment
(QFD), functional strategy
development via, 81–102
additional matrixes done as
required in, 85, 90, 92–94
at B & W Inc., 98–102
documentation in, 85, 94
at Hewlett-Packard, 96–97
hows brainstormed to meet
identified *wants* in, 85, 86–87
measures identified for, 84, 85,
86
relationship set in, 85, 87–90
strategy developed in, 85, 94
success factors in, 97–98
values calculated and priority
rankings set in, 85, 90, 91
Quality, of Management Product,
13–15, 16, 95, 131
see also Total Quality
Management

Raychem, 42
Reengineering, evaluation of, 7–8
Relationships, setting for
functional strategy
development, 85, 87–90

Sales and Operations Planning
(S&OP), 120, 151–59
benefits, 157–59
Pre-SOP, 155–57
process, 152–57
Sales calls, in-context customer
versus, 40–41
Scaled-down approach (Plan B),
128, 130
Service attributes, Kano Model on,
34–35
"Shewhart Cycle," *see* PDCA cycle
Simulation, in Choice Modeling,
50

About the Authors

Tom Wallace is a consultant, author, and educator specializing in Strategic Planning and Resource Planning. He has been an independent consultant since 1972.

Mr. Wallace has authored a number of books, including *Customer Driven Strategy: Winning Through Operational Excellence*, (1992), *MRP II: Making It Happen: The Implementers' Guide to Success with Manufacturing Resource Planning* (1985, 2nd edition 1990), and *The Instant Access Guide to World Class Manufacturing*, (to be published 1994). He currently writes an ongoing column titled "Customer Driven Strategies" *APICS: The Performance Advantage* magazine.

Mr. Wallace has consulted with a wide range of firms on Strategic Planning, Sales & Operations Planning, and Manufacturing Resource Planning. Consulting clients have included Baxter, Cincinnati Milacron, Combustion Engineering, General Dynamics, McDonnell Douglas, Pfizer, Pitney Bowes, Procter & Gamble, Spectra-Physics, and the U.S. Navy. His more recent consulting work has centered largely on executive issues and decision-making processes.

In his 20 plus years of experience, he has developed and presented a variety of seminars on Strategic Planning, Manufacturing Resource Planning, and Purchasing. He has taught over 10,000 executives, managers and specialists in the United States, Canada, and the United Kingdom.

Mr. Wallace holds a Bachelor of Science degree from Marquette University and an MBA from Xavier. He is the president of T. F. Wallace Inc. in Cincinnati, Ohio and is a Distinguished Fellow at the Ohio State University's Center for Excellence in Manufacturing Management.

Bill Barnard is a practitioner and facilitator in Computer-Integrated Decision Making. His work focuses on supporting small to medium size companies in their move to market and customer "balanced" enterprises. Bill now facilitates companies using the processes and tools proven successful at Hewlett-Packard, AT&T/NCR and other companies.

Bill's experience includes the implementation of Quality Function Deployment in strategy planning, and in-context customer research processes that have successfully supported teams in electronics, consumer goods, consulting services, software, network management and strategy planning. Bill is also an early adapter of the successful integration of QFD with deployment assuring processes—derived from *Hoshin Kanri*—a process he calls Strategy Deployment.

Barnard has integrated experience in Manufacturing Operations Management, Industrial Planning, Automation, and Control Systems, and Strategy and Product development; experiences he completed while working for Hewlett-Packard, AT&T/NCR, Revlon and Pitney Bowes. He works worldwide today with clients that include HP, Motorola, Pierce and Stevens (A Pratt and Lambert Company), Senco (a Sencorp Company), Scotsman, Franklin Industries, Modicon/AEG and other U.S. and European-based organizations.

He has a degree in computer science, is certified by the American Production and Inventory Control Society (CPIM), is a Senior Fellow at the Center For Competitive Change at the University of Dayton, and the External Faculty to Motorola University. For over twelve years Bill was a member of the APICS Certification Council and served as a member of the committee responsible for writing the Material Requirements Planning (MRP) exam and was a founding member of the Systems and Technology Certification Exam Committee.